What Heaven Left Behind

by Polly Basore

*What Heaven
Left Behind*

Published by AngelBooks, Bel Aire, KS.
First paperback edition, October 2005.
ISBN: 0-97771749-0-5

Cover photo by Polly Basore.
Cover design by Carlene Williams.
Book design by Larry G. Nichols II.
Printed by Mennonite Press, Inc. in Newton, KS.

Additional copies of this book may be ordered online
 at www.whatheavenleftbehind.com

Please visit www.angelworksinks.org
for more information about the author's philanthropy.

Special thanks to Angie Prather, whose kindness and unyielding
support made this book possible; I don't think I would have found
the courage without you. Thanks also to Nancy Basore, my sister-in-law,
for her careful proof-reading.

"In the end, only kindness matters."

–Jewel

For Henry

Acknowledgements

*E*verything in this book is as true as my memory will allow. Nothing was embellished to make for a better story; it wasn't necessary. If people are named, their real names are used. No characters are combined, nor separate events condensed for the convenience of storytelling. Some people aren't named because I didn't find their names important to the retelling. Others are unnamed because I encountered many whose names I never knew.

If a detail was not significant to me at the time, I did not, as some narrative journalists do, go back to find it out. Rather, I attempt to portray "felt life," or rather my life as I experienced it at the time. I do not intend to represent events as anything more than life from my viewpoint.

If I got something wrong from your viewpoint, I apologize. My best friend and former newspaper colleague Roy Wenzl says we all live our own mythology, and I suspect he's right. Maybe this book represents no more than my myth for myself — that of a woman who wanted to make my life and money count for something.

—PMB

Prologue

I never wanted to be rich. I wanted to be dead several times, but never rich. I had problems money couldn't solve.

People I loved were dying: My father from heat stroke. Fourteen months later, my mother from cancer. I was already divorced; now I was orphaned. Images of my parents' deaths haunted me. I couldn't sleep. I couldn't concentrate.

I often wondered why I was left behind, stuck here in this life with no one to look after me. *I want permission to die*, I thought. *Then the pain will stop*. Then I wouldn't have to take care of myself, or worry that I would try, but fail.

I lost focus at work. I couldn't see the point. Day upon day of meetings, deadlines, budgets. For what? What would I really accomplish between now and the time someone scattered *my* ashes?

Part of me wanted to give up at life, but I knew I couldn't.

It wasn't just me who needed my care. There was Henry, my little boy. And later there was Dorothy, my great aunt.

But I wanted more than responsibility to bind me to this life. There had to be another purpose. What was it?

It wasn't money.

It would never involve money.

Or so I thought.

Chapter One

$\mathcal{I}$ had reached that point in life where the sidewalk ends and there is no more concrete path to follow.

I was 34 years old, a workaholic journalist and a single parent starting over. Years spent chasing big dreams in big cities were behind me; so was marriage. I had just bought a house in Bel Aire, Kansas, a small town on the northern edge of Wichita, where I now worked as an editor at The Wichita Eagle.

The house was what you call a fixer-upper. It looked decent enough on the surface; it reminded me of the home I'd grown up in.

I was raised middle class in Oklahoma, with little knowledge of poverty or wealth (though I did take note that my uncle, the Texas oil man, drove a Cadillac and owned a poodle.) My parents shunned excess and gave generously, their values shaped by the Depression and World War II. The house I grew up in was large but spare. It was brick with four bedrooms and a basement, because we were a family of five and Mom was afraid of tornados.

Looking at my new home, I saw a nice three-bedroom, split-level ranch in a quiet neighborhood on a corner lot with lots of mature trees. The inspector my real estate agent hired saw the truth: Wood rot around the windows. Faulty wiring in the basement. A leaky pipe rusting out a gas line under the house. The house badly needed repairs, fresh paint, new carpet, new appliances. Reading over the inspector's report, I expressed my shock out loud to no one in particular:

Man, someone's going to have to die so I can inherit some money to fix all this!

Words I'd later wish I'd never spoken.

I was so rattled by the contents of the inspector's report that I ran a stop sign while driving away from the neighborhood. A highway patrolman pulled me over and ticketed me.

Dad came over with his tool kit the weekend I moved in. He fixed electrical problems, installed new light fixtures, worked over all the small problems of the house that men of his generation seem to intuitively know how to fix.

He was 78 years old. He'd been abandoned by his father as a young child, during the Depression and Dust Bowl years in Oklahoma. Dad was uncommonly smart, like his mother, who'd earned a college degree in chemistry and found work at the local health department, educating the public about tuberculosis. When World War II came along, Dad signed up for submarine duty with the Navy, hoping to send home extra dollars. When the war ended, Dad had two bronze stars and a way to pay for college. The GI Bill paid his way through a doctorate in electrical engineering from Massachusetts Institute of Technology. He went from there to work as a rocket scientist at a government nuclear weapons lab, then to the State Department, working for President Kennedy on arms control, coming up with the design for the Hot Line between the U.S. and the Soviet Union, the communication device intended to avert accidental nuclear war. In 1967, he returned to Oklahoma State as a professor of engineering, where he worked until he died.

Dad's help on my house was the kind I expected from him. Whenever I'd needed anything, he was soon there. After I'd divorced, he told me, "Remember, I'm only a two-hour drive away." I never expected to inherit any money from him – largely because I never accepted he would die.

But he did, two months later.

It was a scorching July day, and I was at work at the newspaper, discussing with editors and reporters ideas for a story to illustrate just how hot it was. "Hot enough to fry an egg on the sidewalk? Should we try that?" my colleagues asked.

The call came from my father's new wife; she said Dad had been out at his storage unit, going through his old electrical equipment. When he didn't come home for lunch, she found him there, unconscious. At the hospital, his body registered 107 degrees. In the storage unit where he'd been working, police recorded 140 degrees. He was brain dead now, lying in an emergency room bed in a room chilled to bring down his body temperature. When I looked upon him, I shook from shock and fear and cold.

His body was so covered with burn blisters, police briefly considered he'd been the victim of foul play. Investigators eventually concluded the burns were the work of the hot concrete he'd collapsed upon. Tubes ran from his mouth, one inflating his chest with assisted breathing, another suctioning blood from his mouth. His eyes were half shut, vacant when you lifted the lids. Nothing about him looked like my father.

Nothing, but his hands.

His hands were large, strong-looking and tan, with finger nails dirty from work, as they'd always been. After we turned the machines off, I held his hand, disbelieving

I could ever let go.

The next day, newspapers across Oklahoma carried a front-page story about the 78-year-old man who died of heat stroke.

When we read his hand-written will, I was surprised to learn that his assets would be equally divided among my brother, my sister and me.

If I'd ever thought about it before, which I don't think I ever did, I probably assumed that any money Dad had would go to my mother, or to his second wife. And any money he might have had? I assumed it wouldn't be much.

Dad spent his whole life giving away money to people he thought needed it more. He didn't care for things or money at all; he never attempted to make a lot of money and never spent money on himself.

When he and Mom divorced in 1979, he gave her a generous alimony and moved into a cheap efficiency apartment; he stayed there for more than 20 years.

He wore decades-old sports coats, belts and shoes to work. For transportation, he walked, rode an old red bike, or drove one of several old cars he kept running himself, his hands getting caked with grease, sometimes bloodied, cut by tools that slipped. Dad self-mockingly called his lifestyle one of conspicuous *non*-consumption.

Dad enjoyed telling the story of the time a telemarketer called him with a scheme to make him rich.

"But I don't want to be rich," Dad told him. The voice on the phone argued, "Sure you do, everyone does!"

My Dad was insistent: "No. I don't."

He wasn't stingy, though. He was always attuned to others' unmet needs, and gave freely. He had a soft spot for single working mothers supporting families on modest incomes, and first generation college kids. If he encountered someone who really needed something – like groceries, or a car fixed, or a pair of glasses – he'd pay for it. He gave of his time, too, happily pealing potatoes at the soup kitchen, fixing people's TV sets, installing their ceiling fans, repairing their cars, mowing their lawns. He never charged anyone; Dad wanted to be useful, not paid.

People who tried to show their appreciation with gifts were often disappointed; Dad didn't want anything. Gifts he received rarely left their boxes; his tiny apartment grew crowded with the things he didn't need and didn't ask for. Once I gave him a combination magnifying glass and work lamp. He said it was the best gift he'd received in 10 years. I stopped giving him gifts after that; I made donations to charity instead. He liked that.

When he finally moved out of the efficiency, remarried just weeks before he died, the wedding invitation said, "Your presence is requested, but not your presents."

About his estate, his widow explained that she and Dad both wanted it this way; Dad had already taken care of her by paying off her mortgage as soon as they were married. My mother, meanwhile, was taken care of through Dad's retirement benefits that established her as beneficiary upon his death.

Whatever was left would be split evenly among his kids.*

I wondered, what could there be? He had one decent car and two older ones; the storage unit full of dusty amateur radio equipment and other electronics, and a dozen old suits. My sister became the executor — Dad hadn't thought to name one — and went to work. It turned out he still held a mortgage on a rural property, plus some bank CDs and savings bonds.

I ended up with about $50,000.

More money than I had ever seen in my life.

What would I do with it?

What would Dad want me to do?

It felt strange not to be able to ask him.

I wanted to give it away, to someone without a job, a car, or a master's degree. Instead, the first thing I did was pay off the lease on my 2000 Volkswagen Beetle. Dad always paid cash for his cars; it made sense to spend his money paying off mine.

---

* The financial assets were split three ways, but Dad himself was split two ways. He was cremated with his ashes split into two boxes. My brother Paul took one set of ashes home to Australia to scatter in the Pacific Ocean; the other set was buried in the family plot in Douglass, Kansas. (Unorthodox yes, but then my father spread himself thin his whole life.)

Chapter Two

$\mathcal{M}$om was also raised during the Depression in Oklahoma. Her father had a job as a line manager for the phone company. Though times were tight for her family, they weren't poor. The poor families, Mom said, were the ones whose kids came to school without shoes, even in winter.

It was hard to imagine. I always had shoes as a child.

And Mom? She had a whole closet of shoes, the shelves lined with box after box of pumps and sandals and slippers in different colors, for different seasons, occasions, and outfits. Mom liked to shop for shoes. Actually, she liked to shop, period.

In fact the only thing I remember ever doing with Mom outside our house was shopping.

Mom was bright and capable, like Dad. As a teen, she fronted Big Bands as a singer. She went to college on a singing scholarship, studied journalism, and became editor of her college newspaper. She fancied becoming a news reporter, though she set that dream aside when she married my father. Mom possessed a deep faith, once teaching Sunday school and evangelizing for the church. But by midlife, she suffered from depression and agoraphobia, a fear of going out in public. She never went with me to church and rarely came to my school performances. We never went to the movies, the pool, or even the park.

But she did take me shopping on a few major excursions each year: for back-to-school clothes, birthday presents, Christmas presents, Easter dresses. There seemed no better anti-depressant for her. When she shopped, she talked to people, made friends with strangers, listened to sales clerks' personal problems and offered advice. It was a marvel to behold. Mom also shopped from catalogs, chatting up 1-800 operators, making friends with UPS delivery men.

I watched her and tried to make sense of it. There always seemed to be enough money.

Later I realized Mom wasn't really all that extravagant.

Both my parents always bought new, taking care not to buy more than we needed or pay more than necessary. And everything we no longer had need of, we gave away – including a house once donated to church rather than sold to help pay for a new one.

The house I grew up in was nice but modest. The furnishings were nothing fancy; most of it dated back to years before I was born. The outside was rather plain, I thought, with aluminum storm windows that begged for trim.

Mom didn't like it when I came home raving about the house of one of my friends who'd moved out by the Country Club. It was lavishly decorated with features I didn't know existed, like a trash compactor, and a private sink and vanity in the daughter's bedroom. Mom said not to be impressed; the family was deep in debt, spending more than they had.

What's debt?

Mom and Dad both shunned debt. Credit cards in our house weren't for borrowing, only for convenience. Balances were paid in full each month.

Once when I put a prom dress on lay-away, Mom frowned. Lay-away isn't for people like us, she said.

When I was 18, I'd asked Mom for her financial information so I could apply for a college loan, Mom refused to give it to me. My parents had saved for college since the day I was born — as I had been told, time and again — I didn't need aid and I shouldn't borrow, she said.

But what if I want to go some place that costs more than what you've saved?

"You don't need to go to an expensive school; you can get as good an education at a state school as anywhere," they both told me. It was hard to argue that since Dad taught at the local state university.

Beyond their examples and general instruction to avoid debt and take no more than you need, neither one of my parents did much to teach me about money. They wouldn't talk about specifics. I never knew what Dad made nor how much the mortgage was or anything like that.

The time I had my first credit card, I thought the $500 spending limit meant I could spend that much each month. (I quickly learned that is only true if you pay it off each month.)

I went to the local university and came through college with no debt — except for $1,500 I'd racked up on credit cards. Dad paid it off before I got married. I didn't ask him to pay it off, but he did. He said he didn't think I should go into marriage owing money.

When I left my marriage ten years later, I didn't owe any money then either.

My ex-husband and I had lost thousands of dollars on a condominium, which took months to sell after I lost my job in Washington, D.C. But we'd saved money while we were married, invested in the 401k plan at my job, and drove old cars provided and maintained by Dad.

Mom gave me $5,000 to start over. I didn't ask her for money, anymore than I had asked Dad to pay off that college credit card. I didn't turn it down, either. And within two years I went from renting an efficiency apartment, to buying a three–bedroom house. I cashed in the 401k money that had rolled over to an IRA, paid the penalties for early withdrawal and used what was left to make the down payment.

Going through Mom's papers after Dad died, I found a folder labeled with my name. In it was a printout of an instant message exchange between Mom and Dad talking about my new house.

They were both saying how proud of me they were, how great it was that I was being financially independent and hadn't asked them for help with the down payment. They had never said this to me; I smiled to see their words in print.

Chapter Three

*D*ad had been dead a year when Mom gave me a book: "The Courage to Be Rich," by Suze Orman. I hated the title. I was embarrassed to be seen reading a book with such a name.

I wouldn't have read it at all, if it hadn't been for one thing: Mom was dying now. So I did as she asked. I read the book, cover to cover, on the plane home from one of my trips out to visit her.

The book surprised me. It wasn't about being rich at all. It was about getting over the fear of money. I was intrigued.

In her book Suze Orman explains how we are all shaped by our emotional response to money. Many people end up being afraid of it.

Perhaps I was afraid of money. My parents had raised me to regard money with caution; debt was to be shunned, excess was to be shared. And people who focused on making money were not to be trusted. As a result, I never focused much on what I made; I turned the checkbook and bills over to my husband and focused on my work, not my paycheck.

But now I was divorced, with money from an inheritance to manage.

And Suze Orman was offering me concrete ideas for demystifying wealth. What impressed me most was her simple list: "People first, then money, then things." The philosophy matched what I'd been taught, but her book also provided the specific, how-to, financial advice I'd never learned.

Did Mom know?

I decided my finances deserved more attention. I scheduled a meeting with a financial planner. I still had $30,000 in inheritance money but no clear idea what to do with it. The financial planner, Steve, asked me what my goals were.

Goals?

I knew I wanted to save for college for my son, Henry. But beyond that, I honestly didn't really think much about investing for retirement. I figured I would work 'til I died, as my father had done. Money didn't matter to me.

But I took Steve's advice, increased my savings in my 401k plan, bought an IRA and started making monthly deposits in a college savings fund.

Mom's cancer progressed quickly. I went to visit her in a hospice in-patient unit. She faded in and out. Her skin turned gray. I slept on a bed next to her, and sometimes, when I looked over, I thought she looked dead. When I checked her cheek, I found it warm. Relief.

She was eating less and less. During her lucid moments, I told her about Henry. He was 5, and about to start kindergarten. I told her about the financial planner and my efforts to be responsible.

I did not tell her about the $1,500 diamond pendant I'd bought myself for my 35th birthday because I knew my father was dead and my mother was about to be dead and they wouldn't be getting me anything. It felt stupid, silly, selfish and embarrassing.

Neither did I tell her about how Steve the financial

planner had asked me during our meeting if I would be inheriting again. I told him I assumed not, or at least not much, maybe some family farmland.

Years earlier, Mom had written me out of her will. She did it after I was laid off from my job as a reporter in Washington and considered a move to Oklahoma, near my husband's parents.

Mom said I'd be throwing my career away and make myself miserable living in the same town as my in-laws. But I knew she was jealous. My son Henry had just been born, and moving to Oklahoma would place him near three of his four grandparents — everyone but her. She lived in Arizona at the time.

Don't try to run my life, I told her.

I was advised of the change in her will soon after that.

When I received her e-mail saying I was out of the will, I was hurt but simply replied, fine, but please remember how much I love the farm. I asked her directly: *Could I please have the farm someday?*

The farm was 80 acres outside Stillwater, Oklahoma, the college town where I had grown up. The farm meant everything to me. It represented the best of life.

My grandparents, Mom's parents, lived there.

My family visited it frequently. Dad would swing me on the cattle fence gate. Grandma would take me hiking through the prairie flowers. At Easter, we hunted eggs among the forsythia bushes. We took summer picnics in the pecan grove, in a clearing shaded by sun-dappled leaves.

The farm had a barn and a chicken house and mulberry trees and wide open pastures and creeks to cross. But my grandparents were not actually farmers. By the time I was born, they were retired.

In the short span of years that they were alive during my childhood, all I knew of what they did was that Grandpa was a retired lineman from the phone company and liked to go into town and drink coffee.

And Grandma? She sewed — beautiful baby clothes for unwed mothers. And she spent her afternoons working at the mission. I visited her there once. It was a small dark room in a building in a part of town I hadn't seen before. There were stacks of clothing on tables. I didn't get it then. I wondered: *What's a mission? What are unwed mothers and why do their babies need clothes?*

I could not imagine our family ever selling the farm.

Mom did almost sell it. She got an offer on the farm: $40,000, or $500 an acre. When she told me about it, I cried and cried and cried. It cost her $3,000 in legal fees, but she pulled out of the contract and kept the farm. She told me it was worth it to lose $3,000 because she couldn't stand for me to cry, and really, she loved the farm, too.

I didn't think about any of this as Mom lay dying, the cancer giving her pain, the pain medicine stealing her consciousness, and all of it stealing her dignity. I thought only how badly I wanted to stop her suffering, how badly I wanted to stop suffering myself.

I thought of the times we'd fought, how often I wondered if I was a disappointment as a daughter. Couldn't I have done something to keep her from suffering so much depression?

Guilt, sadness and grief ate at me as the cancer ate at her.

I was wrestling with these emotions when my sister asked me to take Mom a form and have her sign it on my next visit to the hospice unit.

Why? What is it?

My sister said the form that would name me as the beneficiary for two of Mom's certificates of deposit.

I was appalled.

You want me to ask a dying woman who can't even sit up to sign a form that gives me money?!

I took the form with me. It lay on the bed where I slept next to her, for what seemed like days. Mom was barely ever awake. I figured it was a nice idea my sister had, but I couldn't ask Mom to sign this form.

Then one of those strange moments arrived that seem to come when someone is dying: Mom was suddenly awake and alert.

We talked more about Henry, who'd just entered kindergarten. I looked at the form, thought about Henry and college, and gathered my courage.

Mom, there's this form.

She said she couldn't possibly sign anything but asked what it was.

I explained straight out that it was a form to put her CDs into my name. Suddenly she sat straight up. She said to bring the form.

"Yes, yes. I want to sign that. ... I need to fix what I did before... It was a mistake." She took the pen and managed a weak but legible signature. Then she looked up at me and struggled for words.

I smiled: *It's okay, Mom.*

Almost as quickly as she had rallied, she faded again and went back to sleep.

In between my trips to see Mom, I tried to prepare

myself for a life without parents. It was hard to imagine. They had always been there for me, with their stories and advice, an answer ready for any question, steadfast supports of whatever I tried to do. To this point in life, I regarded myself as strong and independent, but now confidence was leaving me. I began to realize how many basic things I still didn't know. When colleagues at work teased me for not knowing how often to change my oil or rotate my tires, it hit me hard. In our last conversation, I cried on the phone about it to Mom, a woman dying of cancer consoling her daughter for the last time.

I wasn't there when Mom died, but I felt her dying.

I was sleeping on my couch at home alone and suddenly I heard the sound of labored breath. When it stopped, the phone rang. My sister said Mom was finally gone.

I know.

Mom's will left most of what she had to my sister, but that paper Mom signed put $47,000 in my name. I had the money within a week. Mom also left me the family farmland.

I never wanted to be rich.

Why was it that when people died I got money? All the money in the world wouldn't bring my parents back.

Chapter Four

*W*eeks after Mom died I went to see Aunt Dorothy. I knew little about her other than she was my great aunt — my grandmother's baby sister, a widow with no children who was now 96. The family regarded her as a cantankerous recluse.

Dorothy had called me, saying she needed help.

I found her sitting in an armchair in her assisted living apartment, going through papers.

She was nervously fingering the papers in her lap. I couldn't tell what they were. She had tapes from adding calculators, receipts, hand-scrawled notes, and cancelled checks. There were interest payment receipts from banks, but no statements.

She said she hadn't paid her taxes and needed help. She handed me the papers and thanked me, and I took them and left.

The papers were indecipherable except for one. It listed dividend payments for about 35 stocks. I called my father's older brother, Turley, and asked if he knew what this meant: How much money was there? How far behind was she in taxes?

He said he didn't know; Dorothy wouldn't talk about that to anyone. She didn't have an attorney or an accountant. She rarely used brokers. And she didn't have a will, despite years of family effort to get her to write one.

I didn't know Dorothy well. I had met her only five years before, when I moved to Wichita.

She confirmed her reputation at our first meeting when she made a point of saying, "Now honey, don't feel like you need to come around here visiting me. If I see you once a year, that will be more than enough!"

Dorothy's husband died in 1958 in a plane crash. She managed on her own without any family help until well into her 90s. After I moved to Wichita, she showed little interest in me.

So I was quite startled when I got the first call from the hospital.

I was in the middle of my divorce in 1999. The hospital called to tell me Dorothy was unconscious and jaundiced, and doctors were asking me what to do. I was stunned.

I don't know her at all, and I am supposed to decide her care?

They said yes, because I was her nearest relative. The doctor told me Dorothy had driven herself to the hospital complaining of flu symptoms. She was admitted and her condition deteriorated. Dorothy probably had cancer and frankly was probably too old to treat, the doctor said.

I snapped at him: *Well, if she was healthy enough to drive two days ago, perhaps we should do some tests before we write her off as dead.*

He scheduled the tests. The results showed a blocked bile duct — not cancer — and Dorothy went home to her apartment soon after.

I visited her a few times to see how she was doing.

I found her to be amazing. She lived in a nice apartment

building in a two-bedroom unit. She had the television on CNBC with the stock ticker running across the bottom; Business Week and the Wall Street Journal lay on a coffee table. She liked to read the news and she took an interest in my work in the newspaper. She also took an interest in my clothes, always commenting on my youthful casual attire or my sandals and brightly polished toes.

"I wish I could wear that," she often said.

It surprised me at first, this 90-something woman admiring my toe rings and miniskirts. Dorothy never revealed much about herself but she occasionally dropped hints. She mentioned being wild in her youth, so wild she was "sent away" to a girls' school once. She often mentioned a love of jazz, how she hated the classical music her older sisters played on the piano. When I told her I was getting a divorce, Dorothy made a point of saying that was too bad, "But don't worry, I will never judge you." I told Dad about this. Dad explained that after Dorothy's husband died, she had a live-in male friend for nearly 30 years; Dad suspected that was why Dorothy shut herself off from her family. Shame, or fear of it.

When her health failed again in February 2000, I was in the middle of a custody dispute over my son. I wanted to help Dorothy but I was feeling overwhelmed. I called Dad. *Please come handle this.*

Dad didn't seem eager to deal with her either, but he had a sense of duty. Perhaps he did it for me, as much as for her. I was in a fog, and all I remember is that Dad began making several trips to Wichita to see me and Dorothy. Occasionally I went along.

One visit stands out in memory. Dad and Uncle Turley

were in town to see Dorothy for her birthday, but also to untangle her finances. I paid only passing attention, because this wasn't my problem. But I remember that Dad was asking her where her bonds were, and she started shouting at him, "Get up! Get up! Get up!"

Dad was startled and confused, but obedient. When he stood up, she had him look under the seat cushions. There in an envelope were her state and municipal bonds.

I asked Dad later whether Dorothy had a lot of money. She lived simply, but the stacks of bonds made me curious. He said yes, more than she needs, but wouldn't say how much. I looked at Dad, pleadingly, and asked:

Why doesn't she give some away? There are so many good causes in town, people she could help.

Dad's face fell. He looked down, exasperated, then at me again. "If *you* can ever get Aunt Dorothy to give away her money, do it."

Words I would never forget.

Dorothy was unable to answer my questions about her finances.

I knew I would need help. I called the lawyer who did my will and asked him to meet with her. My lawyer also recommended a CPA who was experienced in untangling the finances of elderly people.

The lawyer drew up a power of attorney so I could go to work straightening out Aunt Dorothy's finances. The CPA said I needed her to sign a special IRS power of attorney as well, to allow myself and him access to her past tax records.

When the lawyer showed up to meet Dorothy, she read over the power-of-attorney form and started screaming.

"I might as well be dead!" she said. Dorothy told us to

leave. "I won't be signing anything today."

This was the Dorothy my older relatives knew all too well: Unpredictable and ferociously independent.

She faxed Turley a note expressing outrage at my intrusion into her affairs. Still reeling from grief over my mother's death only a month before, I gave up.

I sent back her papers with a note: *I am sorry to bother you. I won't bother you again.*

I told Turley that Dorothy was on her own. We speculated that the IRS wouldn't imprison a 96-year-old for delinquent taxes. Yes, I would be there if another health crisis came up, but as far as financial matters went, that was it.

Chapter Five

*M*onths went by.

Or was it years?

In the fog of grief, I couldn't tell the difference.

The death upon death of my parents robbed me of any sense of security. I became afraid. The fear stole my concentration and my memory. I got lost driving my son to school and driving myself home from work.

I stared several times a day at clocks and calendars, trying to reorient myself to the time, the day, even the year. At work I made lists upon lists of things to remember, but still I forgot. Details slipped through my hands without my even being aware.

At the newspaper where I worked, the managing editor asked me why I had not done the annual review of one of my reporters. I swore that I had done it. Then I realized: I thought I had just done it two months before; in fact, it had been two years.

I was chastised by supervisors for lacking focus, for dropping balls. Bosses wondered if I even wanted to be a journalist anymore. I said yes, of course, it was all I had ever wanted to be.

But inside? I wasn't sure.

The grief brought out other symptoms, as well. I awoke at night afraid, drenched in cold sweat. I patrolled the house for threats; I worried that cat toys would hit the pilot light in the hot water heater and start a fire and my young son would die in his sleep. I got angry at the cats, shouting at them for no reason, locking them away in the basement because their attention-seeking meows left me disconcerted. I snarled at grocery clerks when they asked me, "Paper or plastic? Will that be credit or debit?"

Why did everyone demand answers?

What if I didn't know what I wanted?

What if I didn't care?

Why did everyone have to bother me all the time?

Sometimes, when my son was staying with his dad, I took to drinking. This reaction surprised me. I'd made it through high school and college never being much of a drinker. I didn't like the taste, couldn't understand the appeal. And I knew that my father's father had been an abusive alcoholic; my own dad never drank for that reason.

Not until now did I understand why some people drink. Drinking would calm the noise and open the floodgates so the pain would come out. It felt good to let it out, but it was also frightening.

Other times I went spent hours aimlessly shopping – was I looking for Mom at those stores? – and often, I bought furniture. My therapist told me to stop trying to bury the pain by stacking furniture on top. I thought that was funny. It wasn't meant to be. But that's what I was doing: buying large sturdy objects, trying desperately to rebuild the sense of permanence that I lost when my parents had died. I had money but no parents. So I bought furniture.

This went on for some time, a long blur of timelessness, unrelenting pain and unperceived purpose.

Then came a phone call in the night.

It was Dorothy.

"I have no one," she said.

Dorothy was depressed, half out of her mind I supposed, calling me out of sorrow and loneliness. She told me how badly she wished she had someone looking out for her. I told her I would help. Inside, I knew I must.

I know what it's like to feel completely alone.

A day or so later, another call came in the night. My son Henry called out to me from his bedroom. He was crying. He said he hated kindergarten. He said he wondered why he had to be alive, he hated it so much.

I sat up in bed that night and prayed to God. I held my hands upward, gesturing with one for Henry and the other for Dorothy. I pleaded to God:

Help me help them. Help me figure out what to do!

I told God I was sorry I had been so lost in grief that I didn't see the suffering of those closest to me. I asked for forgiveness and help.

Chapter Six

There are days that go by like so many do, where there is nothing but the indiscriminate routine of life, the eating and working and sleeping and slogging along.

And then there are those singular days: The ones where it seems that you live your whole life inside the span of hours. Where everything that you have been, are now, and will become, converges on you.

That day came for me in March 2003.

Getting myself ready for work, I was preoccupied. My ex-husband and I were supposed to meet with my son's teacher that afternoon. We'd asked for a meeting to discuss my son's unhappiness with kindergarten.

I had an idea why Henry was so unhappy.

It all came together for me on a Saturday morning as I watched him try to do work he'd brought home from school. He laid his head on the kitchen table, dragging his red crayon over his paper, complaining that the work was too hard. On the worksheet was a simple geometric design, with instructions to color it according to a code: red for spaces marked one, blue for two, yellow for three. That was it.

It's not hard. How can it be hard? Just get it done. Just get it done and we can do something else.

Henry frowned. He complained. He looked despondent, laying his head on the table. I couldn't understand what was wrong, but my heart began to ache for him.

I tried distraction. I offered to explain square roots.

Henry was just 5, but he'd been asking about square roots after Uncle Turley gave him a calculator. "What's that strange button? What's it for?" Henry wanted to know. His father and I had each told him it was the square root button, it was complicated, and we'd explain it later.

What we wouldn't explain, Henry tried to figure out on his own.

He pressed numbers and buttons on the calculator, working problems over and over. Within days, he had a theory: "It's some kind of division, isn't it?"

So that Saturday morning as Henry sulked, I got out construction paper and started to draw. First, a square. Then four squares inside that one. I showed it to Henry and explained:

Two squares by two squares makes four. The side is the root of the square. The square root of four is two.

I made it bigger. Three squares by three. Four by four. On up to ten by ten.

Henry's eyes grew wide. He smiled and started jumping beside me. He grabbed me around the neck and hugged me.

"OH MOMMY! Why can't school be like this?"

Oh my God.

An image came into my head: Annie Sullivan spelling the word w-a-t-e-r into the hand of the blind and deaf child, Helen Keller, as water flowed from a water pump. How Helen suddenly shook her head in understanding and demanded more words, more words.

I led Henry into another room and got out his blocks.

I stacked two-by-two, then two-by-two on top.

Look, there are eight blocks. Eight blocks stacked this way make a cube. Two is the cube root of eight. Do you understand?

"Yes! Yes!" he said.

With this, my son again became the curious happy boy who loved to learn — the boy who disappeared when Henry started kindergarten.

The next day Henry asked me to teach him something else about square roots. We got out more construction paper. I drew a triangle. Then I drew a three-by-three square against one side of the triangle. A four-by-four square on another side. Then a five-by-five square so that it looked like this:

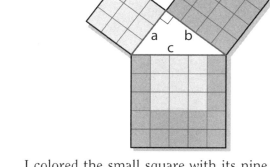

I colored the small square with its nine inside squares yellow and then the medium square with its 16 inside squares blue. On the big square, I counted out nine and colored them yellow, then 16 I colored blue.

See? The yellow and blue squares of the sides equal the number in the big square. This is called the Pythagorean Theorem.

It was a lot to throw at him. I saw his mind working. I asked him if he understood. He didn't answer. He was thinking.

"Why would you want to know this?" he asked me.

I said it was useful for figuring out things. Like how long one side of a triangle would be if you knew the length of two sides but not the third.

Algebra.

I made the next leap.

See these letters? Sometimes they aren't used to spell words, but to substitute for numbers you don't know.

$a^2 + b^2 = c^2$

Henry wanted more. We worked several problems together, me writing out the problems, and Henry finally getting to use that strange button on the calculator to solve for c.

The hypotenuse.

Henry couldn't pronounce it. I told him "hippopotamus" was close enough.

Then Henry surprised me again. He asked me to show him how to solve for b.

Oh boy.

I was getting worn out. My mind was racing. I'd barely gotten through trigonometry in high school. At the rate Henry was demanding to learn, I knew he'd outgrow my ability to teach him within a few years. More urgently, I realized he would never be happy in regular kindergarten. So I'd asked the teacher for help.

Now, it was 9 a.m. and we were supposed to meet the teacher today at 4 p.m. I wondered how to explain it all to her. How could she help us? What could the school do?

The phone rang.

I jumped.

Ringing phones at unexpected times are bad, I'd come to believe. Somebody telling you somebody is dead, or telemarketers. Or so it seemed after getting the calls that Dad had collapsed, that Mom had cancer, that Mom had died. I'd fallen into a habit of shouting at the phones for ringing. I didn't realize how often I did this until I overheard Henry advising a friend not to call our house.

I answered the phone and nearly dropped it.

Aunt Dorothy had collapsed. She wasn't breathing.

The ambulance took her to the emergency room.

A nurse from her retirement home called me because I was listed as her health care power of attorney.

Me?

I drove to the hospital, head spinning.

A chaplain greeted me at the emergency room.

She's dead.

No, she's not dead, the chaplain said. But she wasn't breathing or responsive. She's on a respirator, the chaplain explained.

I saw his lips moving. Felt like I was watching him talk to me from 10 feet away.

Where is she?!

She was about to die, and I wouldn't be there? I was agitated. I asked the chaplain to take me to her. He said he couldn't, she was getting a CAT scan and there was nothing I could do anyway.

I became angry.

Nothing I can do? I can hold her hand while she dies!

Inside my mind were flashes of my father dying in the emergency room, a half dozen of us gathered around him as we shut off the respirator and watched him die, me holding his hand.

Sometimes holding someone's hand is the most important thing, I told the chaplain, my voice pleading. My soul, shredding.

The chaplain nodded but said I had to wait. Just a few more minutes. He offered to get me coffee. I said fine, thanks, and wondered what it must be like to have a job where you get people coffee while their loved ones lay dying.

Before long, Dorothy was rolled back from the CAT scan and into the ER. Colors flooded together as I swooned. Beeping machines filled my ears.

She was my father's aunt, and laying there she looked just as he'd looked.

Dying.

Suddenly there was a conversation about her being non-responsive and whether I wanted to remove the respirator.

I stared at Dorothy.

I looked at the clock. It was 10:30. I wondered suddenly if I would have to spend the day calling funeral homes. I wondered who did cremation. I wondered if Dorothy wanted to die.

I wondered if I would be able to make a decision that would allow some one to die, arrange for the disposition of remains and STILL make the meeting at school by 4 p.m.

Some part of me was trying to hold onto the reality I'd known two hours before, even though now everything was unreal.

I kept thinking I couldn't miss that meeting. That I HAD to be there because my son had been so unhappy and I HAD to fix it. I couldn't let Henry down.

I couldn't let Dorothy down, either.

I didn't understand what was going on with her. She was unconscious. Someone — why does it seem like there are so many people in the hospital and you never really know who they are or what they do — said she had been sedated and it was hard to tell if she would be able to resume breathing on her own or not. Someone else explained that just because she couldn't breathe on her own didn't mean her brain was dead.

The hands on the hospital clocks were erratic. They stood still for what sometimes seemed like hours. Then they jumped ahead hours at a time, in what seemed like seconds.

Aunt Dorothy was moved out of the ER and into ICU. For over an hour they wouldn't let me see her. I was agitated. She was alone. I was alone.

My mind raced. What would I do if she were my child? She needs me to be like a mother. I imagined myself as my great-grandmother, Florence, caring for her baby daughter. What would Florence want for her child?

I imagined telling my uncle that Dorothy had died.

This will mean money for his children, I thought. She'd left no will and he was the closest living relative. I assumed her money would end up with his children.

Then I felt guilty for even thinking about that.

I called into work and explained that I would be late today, because I might have to decide to let someone else in my family die. My boss said not to come in.

I wanted to do whatever Dorothy wanted me to do. But I had no idea what that was.

Impatient, I went past the ICU sign that said "No admittance" and demanded someone tell me what was going on. A nurse pushed me back out the door and asked me to please wait.

The clock was erratic.

It was after noon. Would I call funeral homes today? Do hospitals keep a list? Would I still be able to make that meeting at school? I called my ex-husband. He said not to worry about the meeting; he could handle it.

No, I have to be there.

The nurse came out. She said there had been some trouble. Dorothy had started to come around, but kept trying to pull her breathing tube out. They tied her hands.

When I walked into her room, I saw her half conscious with tears drying on her face. Her hands were in restraints. The breathing tube was down her throat.

I was consumed by the sight of her sadness. I told her I was sorry, sorry that I hadn't been good enough, smart enough to help her the way she needed help. I told her I loved her. That was all I had to offer but that I did love her and I wouldn't let them do this to her, if she didn't want it.

Don't worry. I'll get the tube out. I'll get the tube out.

I called for the nurse. She called for the doctor. He brought the papers.

Do Not Resuscitate.

I read them over, as best I could. I asked the doctor if I understood this correctly, that signing this meant there would be no more breathing tubes, no more attempts to prolong her life artificially. He said yes.

He asked if I was sure.

Yes.

I signed the paper. I looked at the clock. It was after 2 p.m. The nurse removed the tube and left the room.

I took Dorothy's hand.

Told her I loved her.

And waited for her to die.

I have no memory of what happened next. I know the facts of what happened but do not recall being there. In my memory, events pick up at 4 p.m. I am at the school, meeting Henry and my ex-husband. The teacher greets us and says she has assembled a few people for the meeting. I am exhausted.

We are taken to the principal's office where Henry's teacher, principal, a social worker, and another teacher are gathered. Henry is placed into a room next door to wait. He wants to attend the meeting, thinks he should have a say because it's about him, but the principal does not allow it. My ex-husband hands Henry some paper to draw on.

The school people — I am so drained they are not individuals to me at this point — are telling us that they do not think Henry shows any special talent in math.

They say he appears preoccupied during class, is slow to do his work and reluctant to participate. My ex-husband throws angry words. I intervene, appealing to their humanity. I tell them how Henry said he didn't want to be alive because he felt so unhappy with school. How he became transformed when I introduced him to square roots and the Pythagorean Theorem and algebra.

They look at me skeptically. They say they see no compelling reason to test him for gifted education, and that in their opinion, it is bad for children to be removed from mainstream classrooms. Then they ask if perhaps Henry is unhappy because we are pushing him too hard.

I don't need Henry to be brilliant. I need for him to be happy.

I press them further. I tell them that Henry counts to 1,000, sometimes to 10,000 by 10s.

They offer to let him sit in on first-grade math classes.

That's the best you can do?!

My ex-husband gets up to check on Henry. He returns with the paper Henry doodled on and shows it to them:

$a^2 + b^2 = c^2$

100 x 100 = 10,000

$10^2 = 100$

The school people say nothing. And we leave.

Outside, Henry's father and I agree to handle this ourselves. We decide to yank him from the public school and enroll him a private preschool for gifted children. With that, Henry goes home with his father and I head back to the hospital.

Dorothy had inexplicably started breathing again after her tube had been removed. When I returned to the hospital that evening, I found her looking essentially unchanged: seemingly unconscious, eyes half open and unresponsive.

I sat down next to her.

I told her it had been a rough day, but she sure had done well.

I told her about Henry.

I talked and talked, thinking I was really just talking to myself, getting it out. I told her how Henry was really smart, uncommonly smart.

Smart like my father.

My father, the Ph.D. from MIT, government rocket scientist, engineering professor. And Dorothy's most trusted nephew.

"No," Dorothy said, eyes still fixed, just half open.

She was talking?

"No, Henry is smart like his mother."

Chapter Seven

*D*orothy recovered from whatever had caused her to collapse. The doctors never could say what it was. She returned to her apartment at the retirement home and moved, against her wishes, into a different wing.

The director of the home asked me to come in for a meeting. We sat in a small room. It seemed to me to grow smaller as she spoke.

She explained that Dorothy would need a higher level of care now. She asked me to sign papers approving this, and the additional expense.

Why me?

She said I was the only one she'd been able to reach, that I was named on papers in Dorothy's file.

Me?

I asked to see them. My father was named as the primary contact. I was listed as an alternate.

Yes, that is me, but I didn't know.

The paperwork was filled out in my father's hand-writing. So like Dad never to ask, just to presume he knew what was best and to do it.

I read over the papers and told them everything looked in order and that I approved the change in care, but that I really had no legal authority to sign anything financial.

She wanted me to sign anyway.

I hesitated.

I explained that Dorothy signed for Dorothy, that she had not wanted to name me her power of attorney. I told her that I wanted to respect Dorothy's wishes, preserve her sense of independence. That was everything to her.

She told me I was making a mistake. Dorothy was vulnerable. She was, in the director's opinion, no longer fit to manage her own finances. She told me I wasn't doing Dorothy any favors. Instead, I was leaving my great aunt vulnerable.

Ouch.

I signed the papers. Then I called my lawyer.

He remembered how cantankerous Dorothy had been, not wanting to sign anything giving away control over her affairs.

And yet she had named my father? She trusted him, and why not? She always had.

The lawyer outlined options. He said we could move to place Dorothy under a conservatorship – a legal status that states she's not fit to manage her own affairs. We could do this either with Dorothy's consent or without; it would be harder to do it without her consent. She might have to appear in court, the lawyer said. Doctors would have to testify.

I couldn't do that to her.

I called my uncle. He said it was a good idea. I called the doctor. He agreed.

I couldn't do it.

I just couldn't do it.

Her independence was everything.

I couldn't take that.

Weeks went by. I visited Dorothy every other day before work. I usually found her dressed, sitting in her apartment or in the library at the retirement center, reading her Wall Street Journal.

She was always glad to see me.

She would tell me a story about how she needed to take the newspaper back to the front counter because she shared it with "a little man" who wanted to read it, but apparently couldn't – or didn't want to – pay the subscription.

Dorothy told me this same story nearly every day. And I listened every time as though she was telling it for the first time.

The visits were painful.

In my mind I saw her dying. I saw my father dying. I saw her mind deteriorating. I felt mine doing the same. I knew what I needed to do, but I couldn't do it.

Late one night the phone rang again.

It was a nurse at the retirement home. Dorothy had fallen. She'd broken her hip. She was at the hospital now.

Is she going to die?

No, the nurse said. She is comfortable and sleeping. But she will need surgery. You will need to go the hospital and sign papers. And she won't be able to come back here afterward. She will need attendant nursing care.

Am I going to die?

I didn't say that out loud. But it's how I felt inside. I told the nurse I would go to the hospital in the morning. And then I hung up and tried to go to sleep.

I went to see Dorothy at the hospital the next morning. I was relieved to find her awake, looking well.

She was upset about what had happened. She remembered where she was when she fell. That was a good sign, I thought.

She thought maybe she'd fallen because she had eaten an entire bag of Hershey's kisses the night before. This was her theory. The doctors dismissed it because her glucose levels showed nothing unusual when she was brought in, but that was what Dorothy thought. I knew better than to argue.

I told her she needed hip replacement surgery and after that, physical therapy at an attendant care facility.

"Oh?"

Dorothy, I'd learned by now, would often say "Oh?" when she heard something she had not yet decided to accept or agree with.

I said yes, she needed surgery.

She agreed.

I saw an opening and went for it. I said perhaps the time had come to allow me to help her with her finances. I explained she would be in recovery for weeks and someone would need to stay on top of things.

I told her it didn't have to be the power of attorney, the paper she'd seen before. It could be something else called a conservatorship, which meant the court would monitor me.

Her eyes twinkled.

That's a lot of responsibility, she said. You have a job and a young son. That's a lot of responsibility.

She asked if my uncle didn't want to do it.

No, I said.

She agreed. It was time to sign papers.

I called the lawyer immediately, told him Dorothy had agreed to consent to a conservatorship, that I needed papers immediately, before her scheduled surgery the next day.

Who knew what could happen in surgery? He agreed.

He told me we would have to list the size of her holdings and I would have to post bond as a conservator.

I had no idea how much she had; how could I know, if I didn't yet have authority to know?

He said to estimate.

I picked up the papers, brought them to the hospital and asked for the hospital notary to come to the room.

Flashbacks came to me of Mom in the hospice bed, signing papers giving me money. I didn't want to ask Mom to sign then and I didn't want to ask Dorothy now.

I was embarrassed when the notary arrived. I wondered if she thought I was trying to take advantage of Dorothy. I wondered how often she got called to deathbeds to witness wills. What a strange job she had.

The notary asked Dorothy if she knew what she was signing.

Dorothy said yes.

The notary asked if she knew who the papers named to act on her behalf.

"My niece," said Dorothy. She gestured to me.

I felt guilty, terrified and proud all at the same moment. Guilty I was taking her independence, terrified of the responsibility and proud that Dorothy trusted me.

After the notary left, I told Dorothy I needed some basic information about her finances. Before the court would appoint me, we had to estimate how much there was.

Dorothy said she didn't know.

I took a stab at it. I knew she had at least $100,000 in one bank and stock in more than 30 companies. That was all I knew.

About $500,000?

"Okay," she said. So that's what I wrote down.

Then I asked if her taxes were still giving her trouble,

An impish smile spread across her face. She double-crossed her fingers on both hands.

"I haven't paid taxes in two years," Dorothy admitted. "If they want me, they can come and get me."

Chapter Eight

*T*wo days later I was back at the hospital. Dorothy was going into surgery.

She was fairly lucid beforehand, asking me if I didn't need to be at work instead.

They can get along without me. You can't.

I didn't say that, I just thought it. I wondered how the surgery would go, and whether this would be the day she would die. I hoped not.

They wheeled her gurney into pre-op. I asked the nurses if she could wear her wig. Dorothy was proud about her looks, dismayed at what 96 years had stolen from her. With her wig she had a full head of shiny white hair; without it, in her own words, she looked like a witch — all wrinkles and age spots and bare patches of scalp with a few ragged wisps in between.

The nurses smiled and agreed to let her keep her wig.

The wait in pre-op was supposed to be about 20 minutes. Instead it was hours. This day, I heard later, a pregnant woman had been shot by another woman, a rival for her baby's father. Scheduled surgeries were placed on hold as the hospital's surgeons tried to save mother and baby's life. Both died.

Unaware of what was going on as we waited, Dorothy studied her surroundings. She asked me countless questions about what she saw. I dismissed it as dementia and played along. She asked me questions about the medical equipment on nearby walls. What was it? What was it for? She insisted I get up and look, read what was written on it. She asked who made it. I got up and looked. Turned over a device I couldn't identify.

Medtronic.

"Hmm," said Dorothy. "I'll bet they have those in every hospital. Medical equipment companies must do very well."

I stared at her in awe.

She's not demented. She's a genius!

Ninety-six-years old, going in for her second hip replacement surgery and she's studying the hospital for investment ideas. My mind flashed back to the times I had visited her before, her Business Week and Wall Street Journal on the coffee table, her TV tuned to CNBC. I hadn't paid much attention because I didn't care about money; I didn't want to be rich, after all.

But suddenly I realized it wasn't about being rich for her, either.

It was about being curious and brilliant and engaged in what went on around her.

I marveled at her. And then I sat down and held her hand. We both drifted into sleep until the nurse awoke us and said it was time to go.

Dorothy went into the operating room, and I went into the surgery waiting room. It looked like a refugee camp: crowded; large families with pillows and ice coolers of food, hunkered down for the duration. The adults looked pale from exhaustion; the children were bored. All of us, worn down by the extra hours of uncertain waiting.

I watched them, felt their suffering and fear rise up with

my own until I felt my head spinning. I left the waiting room for the brightly lit hall where it was quiet. I leaned against the wall, staring at the cold tile floor.

The hall's quiet was shredded by a woman screaming, "Oh God no! God no!" A nurse quickly rushed the woman past me and into a private waiting room.

I felt sick because I knew immediately: Someone somebody loved was dead.

I felt the woman's grief reaching out like a wave to pull me under. I wanted to leave the hospital. Instead I ducked into another waiting room and waited.

Finally a nurse came to get me.

"Are you Dorothy Tanberg's niece?"

Yes.

I braced myself.

"You can see her now."

She was in the hall, lying on a gurney headed back to her room. She smiled at me, a smile I knew said, "Are you still here?"

Chapter Nine

$\mathcal{D}$orothy moved into a rehabilitation clinic, and I moved into high gear trying to sort out her finances.

My lawyer said I would need to apply for a bond to serve as conservator.

Post bond? Isn't that what criminals do?

The lawyer explained that if I was going to assume responsibility for a half million dollars, Dorothy's estate would need insurance against me taking her money and heading to some tropical island. I laughed and told him I had no interest in tropical islands.

The bondsman came to the newspaper office. He wore a gray suit and a serious face. We went into a glass-enclosed room where he grilled me about my work history, my finances and anything that presumably could make me a flight risk. My curious co-workers looked on.

I told him I paid all my credit cards off each month and that I supervised investigative reporters who put away people who abuse power for a living. I gave an impassioned speech about how I'd devoted a life to investigating schemers who preyed on the weak. I told him I'd even investigated him before our meeting, that I'd found out he sometimes coached Biddy Basketball when he wasn't wearing a gray suit.

Then I wondered if I had overdone it, if I was somehow

compensating for my own self-doubt about whether I was fit to take this on. Truth was, I'd rarely balanced my own check book.

Slowly it hit me. Just how was I going to reconstruct two years of financial data to pay Dorothy's unpaid taxes? I called the CPA my lawyer recommended. He said the first thing I needed was a complete inventory of her assets.

Oh great.

What I had seen of Dorothy's record keeping was a mess. There were assorted check stubs, and a paper I remembered listing about 35-40 stock dividends. And there were bank statements from her four banks.

"Four banks? That's nuts. Why does she have money in four banks?" the CPA asked.

I hadn't much thought about it until that moment. Then I realized the one account Dad knew about had $100,000 in it — the maximum amount the federal government will insure in the event of a bank collapse.

Maybe she has it in four banks to make sure it's all insured.

"What?" the CPA asked. "How many stocks did you say?"

Thirty-five or 40.

He asked if I had ever seen an old tax return for her.

Yes, I have. The last one my Dad did in 2000.

"What was her income?"

Oh between $40,000 and $45,000, I think.

"To make that much money a year off dividends and interest takes assets around $1.5 million."

I nearly dropped the phone.

I turned Aunt Dorothy's apartment upside down searching for financial records. I found the disorganized tax papers in her desk. But then, I took her keys and opened her lock box.

There were notebooks full of rule-lined paper and neat rows written in a bookkeeper's hand with records going back 15 years. There were keepsakes – her birth certificate, marriage certificate, clippings of her husband's fatal plane crash in 1958 and a memorial folder from his funeral.

There was a puzzling series of letters written to the cemetery and funeral home in Great Bend. One made reference to a $75 salvage credit for a casket. It seemed that Aunt Dorothy had dug up her husband in 1976, had his remains cremated and delivered to Wichita. The casket was salvaged for a credit against the disinterment expense.

I guess this is how you become rich; you pinch pennies, even if it means selling your husband's casket for salvage.

She later inexplicably spent $1,000 on a grave marker for the empty grave. Then later, she wrote the cemetery asking what she could do to sell the plot.

Suddenly I recalled a conversation with Dorothy some years before when she mentioned that her husband's family thought he was buried in Great Bend but actually he was in the trunk of her car. At the time, I thought better than to ask her to explain. Now upon finding the series of letters, I understood. Her car had since been sold, and I found her husband Milton in a box in her closet.

That, however, was not the most amazing discovery.

The most amazing discovery was in two manila envelopes marked "A-M" and "N-Z." Each was full of original stock certificates, each with a dated cancelled check attached showing the stock purchase price.

I didn't know it yet, but this was what a million dollars looked like.

You think a million dollars is a bunch of hundreds, stacked in a briefcase, or gold bricks being hauled out of a vault in a bowling bag. But here was a million dollars in the form of stock certificates in two envelopes with "A-M" and "N-Z" written on them in an old lady's hand.

A brilliant, eccentric, independent old lady.

I took all the documents to my car so I could begin building an inventory of her assets. But first a trip to Best Buy for software.

I knew I wanted to build a financial database, but all I found was what you would expect to find: Software for small businesses or basic personal finance needs: tax prep, retirement planning, college saving kind of stuff.

What? No software for How to Track Your Crazy Old Aunt's Millions?

I settled on generic database software for $19.99 and went home to construct my own database.

I'd never built a database before.

But then again, I'd never managed a family fortune either, or until recently, signed a Do Not Resuscitate order.

I was quickly learning it didn't matter what I had ever done before. All that mattered was what I needed to do next.

Chapter Ten

*D*orothy was walking again within a week of her hip surgery; she returned to her assisted living apartment within two weeks. I barely got the stock certificates returned to her lock box before she came home. Yes she had agreed to accept help with her finances, but I wasn't sure how'd she feel about me taking the stocks, and I didn't want to find out.

She worked every day with the physical therapist on walking again. The therapist marveled at her progress, saying she was in better shape than most 70-year-olds. As she worked on knee bends, he told her he was amazed that she didn't complain of the pain.

"I'm too old for that," she said.

My life became a blur. I would take my son to school in the morning, swing by the retirement home to visit Dorothy then head into work, usually late or barely on time. My cell phone rang with calls from social workers and physical therapists. I spent my noon hour visiting banks, financial advisors, the lawyer, the CPA. In the evenings, after feeding my son and helping with his homework, I would sit in front of the home computer and work on the database.

As the details of her finances came together, I realized that the four banks Dorothy had her money in were paying vastly different interest rates, none of them very good. I knew I wanted to consolidate her assets as much as possible, but at a bank with a good rate.

About the time I was considering this, a vice president of one of the banks called and asked if there was anything she could do. I couldn't remember ever being called by a bank vice president before. I was curious. I agreed to see her.

I was instructed to come to the third floor of the downtown bank, to the Trust Department. I dealt mostly with ATM machines, so this was definitely something new. The Trust Department looked like a law office, full of dark paneling and leather chairs and paintings of people riding horses and hunting foxes.

When I arrived, I was offered coffee. I accepted, hoping the coffee would measure up to the furnishings. My financial advisor always served coffee in china with real cream; it was a little luxury I enjoyed. The trust officer brought me coffee in a plastic foam cup with a powder packet.

Sigh.

The bank vice president was a woman. I liked her immediately. She brought along the trust officer who'd made the coffee, and they sat me at a giant conference room table and proceeded to tell me the services the bank had to offer.

I wasn't fully listening because I knew I wouldn't be paying anyone else to do what I felt I could do, but something strange caught my ear and jolted me to attention: The phrase "affluent customer." She'd just said something about how the bank liked to take care of its affluent customers.

I laughed out loud.

I'm not a millionaire; I just play one on my lunch hour.

She said that was a funny line, and asked if I used it with my friends.

No.

I wondered if she often used such flattery on her clients. Truth was, I hadn't told anyone anything about this; too unbelievable, too hard to explain. And anyway, one of the main reasons I never aspired to be rich was that I couldn't stand the idea of being treated differently because of it.

What I really wanted, I told the vice president, was a better interest rate. I mentioned the poor rate the bank was paying now. I asked if they couldn't match the higher rate another bank was offering.

She excused herself and left the room. She returned saying they only did such things for a handful of customers, but yes, the bank would be pleased to match the higher rate if it meant keeping my business. I thanked her and agreed to transfer over all my great aunt's cash assets.

Later I took Aunt Dorothy a computer printout showing the inventory of all her assets. I explained how I had transferred her money to the one bank because I'd persuaded it to give me a higher interest rate that would be worth thousands to my aunt.

Dorothy studied the inventory, giggling with delight. I pointed out the figure at the bottom of the page where it said Total Value Assets: $1.4 million.

She looked up at me in a show of surprise and asked: "Well why am I living here? Why am I wearing this?"

Dorothy occupied a small, modestly furnished one-bedroom apartment in a modest retirement home where she often complained about the décor. The formal sitting room, she thought, resembled a bordello; the hallway walls were decorated with quilts. "Somebody really likes these I guess," she would say with a tone that made it clear she did not.

Her clothes were the same nearly every day. She wore

white orthopedic shoes and white pants and a pink jacket, the uniform she'd worn for decades as a Wesley Hospital volunteer.

Where would you like to live? What would you like to wear?

She waved me off. Dorothy, it seemed, liked to complain far more than she liked to change.

At the end of our visit, I gave her a hug and a kiss on the cheek and made my way toward the door. She called after me, "Now go and make me a millionaire!"

I turned away from her and spoke quietly.

Oh Dorothy, you already did that. I just want to make it count for something.

Chapter Eleven

*D*ion, the top investigative reporter at the newspaper, came up to me full of excitement. A middle-aged man with thinning hair, he was wearing the expression of an eager child.

I was Dion's editor. Dion was ruthless at finding out what people didn't want known; his stories often led to the indictment or resignation of public figures.

Dion and I had just been through a messy mayoral election. Between the primary and the general election, the frontrunner's father died. The candidate was the subject of many stories. Dion and I shared a passion for aggressive political reporting, but we'd also both lost fathers recently; neither of us wanted to kick a man when he was down. It made for a grueling several weeks; the frontrunner lost.

The campaign was finally behind us when Dion came to me, saying he found a story that would allow him to build something up, instead of tear something down.

"I want to save the Colvin Library."

The Colvin Library was a public library branch housed in an elementary school located in one of the poorest areas of town. The city planned to close the branch because it would save $17,000 a year.

As a journalist, I knew I was supposed to be objective.

I'd been objective for years as a Washington reporter,

training myself not to form opinions, much less express them. I was objective through the 1990s as Congress refused to provide universal health care, failed to fix spiraling entitlement costs that jeopardized Medicare and Social Security, and then "reformed" welfare so that single mothers would be cut off of welfare and forced to work. Objectivity was so ingrained in me that when I would visit extended family over the holidays, and they would ask me what I thought of what was going on in Washington, I would present both sides as I always did in my stories.

But when Dion told me about the Colvin library, I wasn't objective, I was angry. The city managed to find millions of dollars to subsidize private businesses in the name of economic development, but with dubious results. Yet repeatedly, city leaders gave short shrift to the poor.

In the previous year, the former mayor had suggested desperate times called for desperate measures: Since Sept. 11, the decline in air travel had led to the layoff of 15,000 of Wichita's aircraft workers. Some experts said Wichita was economically hurt worse than any city in America — worse even than New York. The mayor suggested taking $1 million from the city's reserves to help the United Way, the local soup kitchen and food bank meet the tremendous needs of the unemployed. The City Council voted it down; twice.

Now the city planned to remove thousands of books from the elementary school as part of its plan to shut down the public library's branch there. Thousands of books would be taken out of a school where immigrant children living in poverty were trying to learn how to read English.

I smiled at Dion.

Yes, Dion. Let's save the library.

Dion persuaded a local official to ride a bus with him,

a long bus ride showing how difficult it would be for the people served by the Colvin Library to travel to the closest other library, the main branch downtown. Dion did this because he knew that the people in that neighborhood did not own cars.

Readers were appalled. Some folks started a save-the-library campaign to raise money to buy books to replace the ones that city had already removed. The school held a read-a-thon, getting donors to sponsor them for books read. Dion joined the read-a-thon and I sponsored him for $50, knowing that objectivity was behind us now. Dion was startled. He thought $50 was a lot.

There weren't many days spent saving libraries. It felt good. So good that I started realizing how bad it felt the rest of the time.

Chapter Twelve

Dorothy had more than a million dollars, but no will.

And as long as the conservatorship was in place, there could be no will. There were no heirs expecting anything. She was childless. Her closest living relative was my uncle, who'd already drawn up a legal document saying he wanted no part of her affairs and no part of her money.

Responsibility for the money fell to me. I kept looking over my shoulder for someone older and wiser to tell me what to do.

No one was there. No one except the memory of my father saying, "If you can ever get Dorothy to give away some of her money, do it!"

I asked Steve, my financial planner, how much did Dorothy actually need? He said that even if she lived another five years and spent the entire time on a luxury cruise traveling the world, she couldn't spend it all.

I knew if she died now, about a quarter of a million would go to taxes. Dorothy wouldn't like that. I didn't like it.

I started thinking, running numbers, trying to come up with an estate plan for Crazy Old Aunt with No Will, No Heirs and Too Much Money. (They don't make software for that, either.)

Steve suggested I look at a charitable donor fund.
Huh?

It's a fund, he explained, where you make a lump sum contribution to a fund, get the tax break immediately, the money is invested according to your wishes, you pay no taxes on the fund's growth, and you get to make decisions about how to dole out the money over time, to the charities of your choice.

You mean I can set aside money for charity now, without having to immediately decide which charities benefit? And forever shield that money from estate taxes?

"Yes."

Steve and I also looked at "529" plans, tax-shielded college savings accounts that Dorothy could set up to benefit her 12 great-grandnephews and nieces. I knew they were all smart kids like Henry, and investing in them seemed like a great idea.

I drew up the proposal to take a significant portion of money and set up the charitable donor fund and the college savings accounts, and presented it to my lawyer, who in turn presented it to the probate judge.

I waited days for an answer.

Stress at work bore down on me. Supervisors said I lacked focus, didn't seem engaged. I dissolved into tears at my desk. Crying, I told my supervisor that I didn't want to just be about tearing people down, that I wanted to build things up.

For the first time, I told him my aunt was a millionaire and I was responsible for the money and I was trying to set up a charitable fund.

Wouldn't it be great if I could do that? If I could give a library money for books or hungry people money for food?

I was sure I sounded delusional. I imagined the boss saying, "See the crazy woman crying in the office, the one who says her 5-year-old understands the Pythagorean Theorem and her great aunt is a millionaire. See the crazy woman who wants to save the world when we just want her to get her staff reviews done on time."

But my boss was a good man. He didn't say any of those things. He just looked at me and said, "You can't let anyone else define who you are. You have to decide."

Really? Sniff, sniff.

My lawyer finally called. The judge said no.

Conservators are supposed to conserve assets, not give them away, the judge said. And besides, what if Dorothy needed an organ transplant someday?

An organ transplant at 96?

That's irrational. Why would the judge say that? Why can't I do this one thing to protect my great aunt's estate from taxes and do some good? I demanded to know.

The lawyer said the judge had never faced a case like this before, and that judges are elected in this county. Perhaps, my lawyer supposed, the judge didn't want some investigative reporter from the newspaper coming back and asking later, in a story on the front page, why he'd let a conservator give an old woman's money away.

Chapter Thirteen

The words of Joseph Pulitzer, founder of Columbia's Graduate School of Journalism, appear on a bronze plaque in the lobby of the school's building in New York: "Our republic and its press will rise or fall together."

I saw these words every day for the year it took to earn my master's degree. I took the statement to heart, along with the ethic imparted by my professors, nearly all of whom had already spent decades in the field: Journalism is not a job, it is a calling. We are guardians of the public trust. The republic depends upon us.

I graduated in 1991, carried with me Pulitzer's words on a key chain, and learned almost immediately that not everyone shared this view.

With readership and circulation in decline, newspapers across the nation were closing. A glut of journalism grads competed with experienced journalists. Jobs were hard to find.

I moved back to Oklahoma, took a job as a city hall reporter at The Tulsa Tribune. Within a year, the hundreds who worked for the paper became jobless as that paper shut down and ceded its competition for circulation to its morning rival, The Tulsa World. I took it as a stark lesson: If a newspaper can't make enough money to survive, its journalists can't accomplish anything. No paper, no defense of the republic.

During my fifteen years in journalism, I watched it happen time and again as newspapers struggled to hit the profit targets Wall Street set for them. We were not journalists but FTEs — operating costs to be trimmed in order to bolster profit margins, and ultimately, stock prices. Hundreds of people I knew were laid off, downsized and bought out. I experienced all three. Somehow I kept landing on my feet; I had friends who were not so lucky.

When I became an editor and moved into management, I wrestled every day with the strain of these cutbacks. Editors were asked to squeeze more and more work from fewer and fewer people, and we were to take on more work ourselves. Most of my reporters had families and children, and I always made it clear to them that families came first. But we all understood that long days and late nights were part of the deal; how else to save the republic?

Yet there were times, as I watched the moms and dads who worked for me stay past their children's bedtimes, an image passed through my mind of children streaming into the newspaper office, demanding, "We want our Mommies and Daddies back!" My own supervisors struggled, too. One admitted that her 3-year-old had announced, "My Mommy lives at the Eagle."

Were we working for the fate of the republic, or the fate of the stock? In reality, I knew it was both. But what about the fate of our families?

After my parents died, I started to question everything, including if the job I was doing was worth it. Most people are just thankful for a job to pay the bills and feed their families. I wanted more. And I was starting to wonder if I didn't have options.

While I was wrestling with this, the top editor

announced to the staff that the newspaper was again struggling to meet its budget targets. To avoid another round of buyouts or layoffs, management would allow employees to take unpaid leave, if they wanted.

I followed the editor into his office immediately after he made the announcement. I asked for four weeks off. As soon as possible.

After some discussion about whether the paper could afford to let me go, my request was approved. I was required to fill out paperwork listing the purpose of my leave.

I wrote this down: *Restore work/life balance.*

My last day of work in the newsroom before my scheduled four-week leave was Friday, June 20, 2003.

I never went back.

Chapter Fourteen

Two weeks into my leave, I vowed to face down my fears.

It was the Fourth of July, a date that coincided with the miscarriage of my first pregnancy several years before, my father's death in 2001 and my mother's cancer diagnosis in 2002.

I bought ingredients for a flag cake — blueberries and strawberries, pound cake and whipped cream. I got myself a shirt imprinted with the image of flags, and for Henry, patriotic decorations for the wagon he planned to ride in a small neighborhood parade.

We were about to leave for the parade when the phone rang.

I answered it. And crumpled into tears on the floor.

Dorothy had stopped breathing, collapsing into her breakfast at the dining table. An ambulance was taking her to the emergency room.

I called my friend Roy, who was also a neighbor.

I was sobbing.

Don't make me watch someone die again.

He was calm. He told me I needed to go. Dorothy needed me.

Of course I would go. But first I called my ex-husband, told him to come get Henry and the wagon.

Don't let him miss the parade.

I'm not sure why it was so important to me that Henry go to the parade, but it was.

I arrived at the hospital, traumatized.

I can't really say what happened next; I don't remember much except for the sound of beeping machines, the smell of floor sanitizer. The feeling that I would die. The machines were loud. I couldn't see, couldn't understand what was going on. I was flooded with flashbacks, transfixed on the image of tubes coming out of my father's mouth, draining blood as he hemorrhaged from the ravages of heat stroke.

I didn't know what was wrong with Dorothy. The staff didn't seem to be doing much for her, nor talking to me.

I wanted to hold her hand, but I was immobilized. I sat on the floor outside her room, feeling dizzy, panic rising within. I waited hours for some word but none came.

Finally I asked to see a chaplain. After another hour, the chaplain arrived.

I tried to explain the grief, the post-traumatic-stress disorder, the flashbacks. The death, the death, the death, how it hurt so bad I wanted to die, too.

The chaplain asked what she could do.

Let me leave. Please, can I leave?

Of course, she said. The chaplain agreed to find out if there were any papers I had to sign before I went. She said she would call me when something was known.

I went home, threw cold water on my face, and pulled it together for my son, who said it sure was hot at the parade. If it wasn't so hot he'd have liked it better, he said.

Yes, I hate the heat, too, Henry.

Later, the chaplain called. She said Dorothy was stable. The doctors didn't know why she'd collapsed, but she'd been transferred to a room upstairs.

I thanked her and took my son to see the fireworks.

Chapter Fifteen

I avoided Dorothy after that. Instead of visiting her every other day as I had been, I struggled to make it at least once a week. She was out of the hospital within days of her collapse, and I realized this could go on for sometime: I would keep getting phone calls, summoning me to the hospital to wait her out on whether she lived or died.

People with post traumatic stress disorder suffer from a sense of reliving their trauma. In my case, I actually was living it over and over, with no end in sight.

I needed to get away from Dorothy. But how? I loved her and she needed me.

My sister suggested I hire a caregiver. We'd hired caregivers for Mom. It took pressure off us, and we saw that Mom preferred receiving care from someone hired to do it rather than her children.

I hired Tommie. She was a spirited woman in her early 60s who I suspected could stand up to Dorothy.

Tommie started visiting Dorothy every day for an hour or two, Monday through Friday. At first Dorothy resisted, saying, "I don't have anything to say to you. You can just sit there and read." But Tommie won over Dorothy in a week, and Dorothy started affectionately referring to Tommie as "my babysitter."

With that solved, I started preparing for my return to work.

My four weeks were nearly up and my supervisor asked me to lunch. I put on a brave face. I talked about how I was eager to come back and start planning coverage for the 2004 elections. I found myself saying what I figured I was supposed to say.

He said that was good because the top editors would be watching me closely. They were concerned about my commitment, especially given my request to take four weeks off. My time off had created a hardship for the staff, after all.

Oh?

I kept on the brave face until lunch was over. I went home and then I went in the kitchen, took a bottle of wine from the refrigerator and started drinking. I broke a glass against the sink and used it to cut my hand, then my arm.

I was alone, stunned and sobbing. Henry was staying with his dad.

Roy, my work friend and neighbor, called to see how the lunch went.

Not good.

He came over immediately and found me drunk and bleeding. He listened as I poured out my pain.

They think I am no good.... It hurts so bad. It hurts so bad. Why does it hurt so bad?

He made me call a suicide hotline. I didn't want to, but I did. I had to explain yes, I cut myself but no, I don't want to die. Not really.

I just want the pain to stop.

Chapter Sixteen

I visited a psychiatrist the next day.

I told her that yes, I thought a lot about dying. I told her about getting lost on the way to work, forgetting things constantly, nightmares with cold sweats, panic attacks and dizzy spells. And the way I seemed to scream and curse the phone every time it rang.

She placed me on mental health leave.

I spent many days feeling numb, sitting on the swing on my back porch and wondering if I would ever feel safe again.

I read books searching for insight.

David Eggers' "A Heartbreaking Work of Staggering Genius" put words to how I was feeling: In his story of losing both parents to cancer in a short time, then taking over his young brother's care, Eggers describes losing days the way some lose pencils.

Sarah Ban Breathnach's "Something More" brought comfort. She told me that life is shaped by all the little decisions, and if you want to, you can completely change your life in less than a year. (She was right, but I didn't know it yet.) What intrigued me most was a quote she used from philosopher Joseph Campbell: "We must be willing to get rid of the life we've planned, so as to have the life waiting for us."

What is waiting for me?

One August night, the phone rang again.

Dorothy had collapsed again. She'd been admitted to the hospital. The nurse told me no, she wasn't about to die, and yes, she was asleep.

Good. I'll be there in the morning.

I pressed the doctors for answers. Why did this keep happening? They ran tests. Lots of tests. Dorothy had congestive heart failure. Her oxygen absorption was low. It was possible she'd had a mild stroke, but test results were inconclusive. And she had injuries from her latest fall. She would need to go into a rehabilitation clinic again.

Otherwise Dorothy was alert. I explained everything. She was disappointed not to go home, but she cooperated. She stayed in rehab for weeks; she enjoyed the attention she got there, as well as from her regular visits from Tommie.

I was glad to have her settled because the one-year anniversary of Mom's death was approaching.

Mom had always said she wanted to be cremated and have her ashes scattered in the Catalina Mountains outside Tucson. Mom lived there many years before moving into my sister's house outside Atlanta, where she died. Mom loved the desert, loved sitting outside, drinking tea, and staring at her mountains, as she called them.

When Mom died, we had her cremated. But my sister and I couldn't then face the trip to Tucson. We agreed to do it on the first anniversary of her death, September 17, 2003.

My sister and I met in Tucson. She brought Mom in a suitcase — a carry-on because my brother had briefly lost Dad's ashes when the airline misplaced his checked luggage.

I took Mom's ashes out to the balcony of the resort where we were staying and placed them on a chair next to a cup of Mom's favorite tea, Constant Comment.

Mom's sister drove down from Phoenix to meet us. We picked up Mom's best friend from Tucson and the four of us headed for Sabino Canyon. The canyon is part of a national park so we kept Mom in a backpack, lest someone try to stop us from fulfilling her wishes.

It was hot. We rode a tram up the mountain and the sun beat down. I thought I would pass out.

Why does it have to be so hot today?

We found a good spot and agreed that we would take turns saying something and scattering Mom's ashes down a ravine. I went first, climbing up on a rock and shaking the ashes from the plastic bag that contained them.

My sister stopped me, alarmed.

The wind was blowing the ashes back into the faces of our aunt, and Mom's friend. I realized what happened, then noticed a feeling of grit in my teeth.

When I returned home from Tucson, time was almost up on my mental heath leave from work.

I felt in no way ready to go back to the newspaper. Hearing this, my psychiatrist gave me bad news. She said she could not justify another extension of my leave. I was too functional.

Too functional?

Yes, she said. I was ably caring for my son, managing my household and juggling my aunt's affairs. There was no reason I could not go back to work.

I told her I was terrified to go back. I couldn't handle those incredibly long hours and intense pressures, and take care of myself and my son and my great aunt, too.

She said she only wanted me to work 20 hours at first,

and never more than 40.
Oh. Sure. I can handle that.

Chapter Seventeen

My request for a 40-hour work week was denied.
No, that's not true.

My request to return to my old job as political editor of the paper at 40 hours a week was denied.

"We can't have that, not when we're going into a presidential election year. It wouldn't be fair to the other editors who would be called on to take up the slack," I was told. "They've already done so much in your absence."

Yes, I know it was hard for them.

I was offered a 40-hour job as a copy editor. Copy editors worked at night, from 4 p.m. to 1 a.m. As a single mother with a 6-year-old, I knew there was no way I could take that job.

Let me think about it.

I'm not going to tell you what happened next because I wish it had never happened. Let's leave it as I ended up drunk and bleeding again, despondent and fearful, feeling like a trapped and injured animal. I was grief-stricken.

Now not only were my parents dead, so apparently was my career.

I can't be what they want me to be. I'm not good enough.

All because I couldn't shake the pain, couldn't concentrate, couldn't do that job and be caregiver to my son, a 96-year-old woman and myself.

I was despondent. I was angry. I wanted to quit. I wanted control.

Quitting seemed self-destructive. After all, what would I do next? I had no idea. But I recalled Joseph Campbell's lamentation: "We must be willing to get rid of the life we've planned, so as to have the life waiting for us."

I'd been managing Dorothy's finances for nearly six months. I expected no money from her — and if there ever were to be any, it wouldn't be soon, I thought. I had watched her nearly die and come back to life, like a wilted flower fading and reblooming. It happened so many times it became my running joke with the hospital nurses who also marveled at her recoveries: "You couldn't kill Dorothy with a nuclear bomb."

But in the time I managed her finances, I got a much better handle on my own. I'd made an inventory of my own assets, knew my net worth, realized that I had options. Maybe I could quit.

There wasn't much that was liquid, though. Not enough to make me comfortable. I stared at the line on a printout of my inventory: Farm, 80 acres, estimated value $40,000.

Sell the farm? Am I nuts?

I went online and looked up real estate companies in Oklahoma where the land was located. I found a number for a firm that specialized in rural real estate, called up and asked them about land values in the area. She said prices were running between $1,500 to $2,500 an acre.

Come again?

The realtor repeated it. My land was worth three to four times what I thought it was worth.

Are you sure? Because I am about to make a major life decision based on this.

She said worst case scenario would be $1,000 an acre.

And with that, the thing I thought I could never do became the obvious thing to do: I would sell the land and buy my freedom.

I called the newspaper and made an appointment to come in and sign my letter of resignation.

I was happy. I was in control. I was free.

I met briefly with my reporters to tell them goodbye.

Many offered me hugs. Dion, my reporter who'd saved the Colvin Library, looked at me and cried.

Chapter Eighteen

When I was very young child, I took swimming lessons at the university where my father taught. The college had an Olympic-size pool and diving well with what I perceived to be a 20-foot-high diving board. (I am sure it wasn't that high, but that's what it felt like.) My father was there watching the day our class was to take turns jumping off the high dive. He'd already spent countless hours with me just getting me to jump from the pool's edge into his waiting arms in water that was only three–feet deep. And now, I was supposed to leap off the high dive.

I climbed the long ladder to the top, frightened and yet enticed by the possibility of being so brave.

I gripped the texture of the board with my toes as I slowly made my way toward the edge. The board seemed to loom over sky and nothingness. I could not see the water below until I reached the edge. When I came to the edge, I concentrated on holding my breath. I was scared, but somehow with Dad looking on, I felt safe. And then I jumped.

I told this story to my husband decades later as I tried to explain why I felt the need to get divorced, to find a different life for myself, even though I didn't really know yet what that life was. He looked at me and said with a gentle kindness that surprised me, "When people see you, they will say, 'That girl sure can jump.' "

I was jumping again now.

I hoped Mom and Dad were watching. From somewhere.

My lawyer called. He said we had a problem.

The bond issued under the conservatorship would only protect my aunt's assets up to $600,000. The inventory I prepared for the court showed she had in excess of $1.4 million.

Nothing's going to happen to her money, I assured him.

Inside I thought how bad this could look to someone who didn't know me, who didn't know I didn't want her money. Here I had just been on mental health leave, and now I've quit my job. And I am asking for someone to trust me with all this money, just on my word?

Not surprisingly, my word alone was not good enough.

My lawyer said we should either apply for a bigger bond, or rescind the conservatorship.

Can we do that?

Dorothy entered the conservatorship voluntarily, he said. She has the option to rescind it. She could sign a durable power of attorney instead. If she did that, there would be no need for a bond or court oversight.

She could also do a will, I realized. And the judge would no longer be able to prevent me from setting up a charitable fund.

Let me think about it.

I wasn't sure I even wanted to ask her. When we'd asked Dorothy to sign a power-of-attorney form before, she'd read the document and shouted, "I might as well be dead." But that was before. Now she trusted me. She told me so over and over, how bright she thought I was, how responsible. She'd told me I should take whatever I wanted for myself, that I deserved it. I told her all I wanted was the chance to do something good.

We talked about what would happen if she died without a will, how the state of Kansas would divide her money among her relatives.

It wasn't as I thought, all going to Turley's kids. My lawyer said it would be spread throughout the family.

I made reports showing who the relatives were, including photos from family Christmas letters I'd received. I included a breakdown of names of the extended family members and offspring of her late husband's family, who wouldn't get anything if she didn't make a will.

Dorothy looked at the information I had gathered listing all the family members of her nieces and nephews and sunk back in her chair.

"A person can't hide, can she?"

Dorothy said she didn't want the state to give money to family members she didn't know. So I told her that if we signed papers replacing the conservatorship with a power of attorney, she could decide where the money went.

She agreed to sign the POA.

Dorothy was fading; I felt a sense of urgency to do something with her estate before she died. Draw up a will. Get the money that could go to taxes into a charitable fund.

But whenever I would try to get Dorothy to consider her wishes for a will, she became agitated. She started saying that she didn't really have that much money and wasn't it all going to go to taxes anyway?

One day, she started crying about it. "I hate this!" she said. I took a deep breath and decided not to bring it up again. It wasn't worth it to see her so upset.

But I couldn't shake the idea of setting up a charitable fund. I could do that on my own as her power of attorney.

I called Steve, my financial planner, and asked him to draw up the papers placing a quarter of a million into a donor-directed charitable fund. Before I signed those papers, I went to see Dorothy.

Tommie was there for her daily visit. Dorothy was in good spirits. I sat down by the side of her armchair in her assisted-living apartment, holding her hand and looking into her eyes as I had done countless times before.

Dorothy, you've got too much money.

"I have?"

Yes. We need to give some of it away so it doesn't go to taxes.

"Okay."

I didn't know if Dorothy really understood what I was talking about at the moment, but I treated her as if she did. I told her how much she had, how much would go to taxes, and what the benefit would be if we placed it in this fund instead. How we would get a tax break up front, how the money would grow tax free in a mutual fund, and how that would keep her estate from paying federal taxes.

She nodded: "Sounds good."

I looked at Tommie to see if she understood the significance of the conversation. I wondered inside if anyone would ever sue me for giving my great aunt's money away and if Tommie would be called to testify.

And then, just as I had looked out over the diving well to see my father's face before I jumped off the diving board, I glanced back into my memory and saw Dad. He was telling me, "If <u>you</u> can ever get Dorothy to give her money away, do it."

I left Dorothy and went to the sign the papers setting up the account, then to the bank to wire $250,000 to the fund company.

It had been so hard for so long, but in the end it was simple: Two signatures from me, and a quarter of a million dollars became forever forward reserved for charity.

Just like that.

Chapter Nineteen

If I could tell the world just one thing
It would be that we're all okay
And not to worry because worry is wasteful
And useless in times like these.
I will not be made useless.
I won't be idled with despair.

Singer Jewell's lyrics to her song, "Hands," reached out to me. I had no idea what I was going to do. I was divorced. My parents were dead. And now, so was my career. I felt disconnected from everything about my life I'd ever known, save my precious son Henry. I had no idea what I was going to do next, but I knew this: I would not be idled with despair.

I will gather myself around my faith
Because light does the darkness most fear
My hands are small, I know
But they're not yours they are my own
And I am never broken.

Well, that wasn't true: I was plenty broken. Shattered, like the glasses I had broken, with shards of pain still wedged deep. But Jewel's song reminded me of the woman I wanted to be, and that was a place to start. I bought her CD and played it over and over and over.

We will fight, not out of spite
Because someone must stand up for what is right
Cause where there's a man who has no voice
There ours shall go singing.

I started volunteering for the local holiday relief program. I signed up people who needed food, clothes and toys so they could have a Christmas. And in doing so, I saw deep into the faces of the poor.

Many were living on a few hundred dollars a month, the frayed safety net provided by welfare for single moms and the disabled. Others relied on wages of not much more, earned at service industry jobs where they made minimum wage wiping tables or busing dishes. They brought their children and their elderly, their mentally ill and their physically infirm.

They approached me nervously, wondering if they would fail some test of need, if I would turn them away, and if they would have to tell their children that Santa did not exist.

And I would smile and say, "Sit down, don't worry, we can help you."

I would tell them that I didn't have a job either, that I had a little boy, too, and aren't children a blessing? And yes, good health insurance is hard to come by when you are out of work.

They would smile back. And I began to feel joy grow inside me again.

In the end, only kindness matters.
In the end, only kindness matters.

Their faces stayed with me. So many people working so hard to survive. Dorothy knew about them, too. She read the newspaper and saw a story about thousands of people standing in line, waiting hours in the cold just to get a box of food for the holidays. "It's bad out there, isn't it?" she asked me.

Yes, it is, I told her, but there are good things happening, too. I told Dorothy how many were trying to help, that Wichita was a good town that took care of people in need.

I will get down on my knees and I will pray.
I will get down on my knees and I will pray.

In my alone hours, I did a lot of praying. I wondered what I could do about all this suffering. How could I help? I had a lot of ideas, but nothing was taking shape.

When I quit the newspaper I thought I wanted to write. I'd always wanted to write. I wondered if I could write stories that could somehow help the poor. I wondered if I could become a freelancer and write stories for my old newspaper.

But the newspaper didn't want me writing stories about groups I was helping. So which would I do?

Write stories about the suffering?

Or try to help them myself?

I started researching local charities, figuring whatever I learned could be useful either way. I researched their financial records, their missions, and the makeup of their boards of directors. I made a list of groups whose work appealed to me, wrote down their tax ID numbers, which I would need if I decided to make a contribution from the charitable fund I'd established.

I wanted to do something big, but I didn't want anyone

to know. I was still incredulous that the fund even existed and wasn't sure what anyone would think. I felt a bit like Robin Hood, as though I'd somehow robbed my rich aunt to help the poor. I wasn't ready to deal with that publicly. Certainly not while Aunt Dorothy was still reading the newspaper.

I decided to make a $10,000 donation to the food bank, which supplied the local soup kitchen and relief agencies with food. The food bank, I knew, could buy $100,000 worth of food with $10,000 of money.

Jewel's CD was playing while I sat at my home computer and prepared to make the donation online.

In the end, only kindness matters.
In the end, only kindness matters.

First, I decided to call up the food bank's website to double check some information. There I found a photo of a wealthy local businesswoman and a story describing how she and her friends raised $25,000 for the food bank. It reminded me of the photos I'd seen in the society column of our newspaper of wealthy socialites helping the poor by holding fancy parties, auctions and golf tournaments.

What do they really know about the poor? Do they do it for the poor or themselves?

The photo triggered something inside me, a feeling I later regretted when I got to know that same business-woman as a person and not just a photograph; I learned her generous spirit was genuine and rooted in authenticity.

But at the time, it caused me to rethink my donation to the food bank. I would not donate $10,000 anonymously.

I would make it $25,000.

Chapter Twenty

*M*arch 1990.

Dad drives us north from Washington, D.C, through Maryland, into Delaware along the coast line, looking for a beach. I am 22, and I have never seen the ocean. I'd spent the first 21 years of my life in a college town in Oklahoma; I hadn't seen much of anything. But I had big dreams, dreams of seeing the world, saving it even, if only I could figure out how. Those dreams had brought me to Washington, where I was working at USA Today, "on loan" from a small paper in Indiana, where I'd left behind the small town and my new husband so I could go live in the big city. Dad supported my dreams, though he often told me you save the world at home; it isn't out there, it's here, in the people around you.

He wanted me to see the ocean, so he flew up to Washington and rented a car to drive me. By the time he was 22, he'd lived at sea for nearly four years, serving aboard a submarine in the Pacific during World War II. Dad loved the ocean as much as he loved the universe and God and all that was expansive and mysterious and which begged to be explored by a curious mind. He loved it so much that we would later scatter his ashes in the Pacific, my brother Paul taking them to his home in Australia, paddling offshore in a kayak and tossing them out to the waters, watching as they sparkled with sunlight before sinking into the waves.

Dad was driving us through rural Delaware, along a winding two-lane road where you could see what it was you were driving through and by. I stared out the window, wondering what it would be like to live near the sea. It was nearly Easter, and in the trees, brightly colored objects blew in the breeze.

What is that?

Sometimes it takes a while to recognize what's right in front of you when it's unfamiliar, when it's something you have never seen before. Hanging from the branches, I finally discerned, were plastic Easter eggs. It was beautiful.

I was getting eager to see the sea. I wanted to stop. Dad drove on, looking for the right spot. Eventually he found a pull-out where we could park and walk. I could hear the sea before I could see it, its tremendous thunder lapping against the sand. It was March and the wind was strong and the air was damp and cold.

We walked between scrub grasses that grew up from the sand, toward the surf and stared. A memory flashed into my mind, and I told my father about it.

In Oklahoma, the only waves were in wave pools in water parks. I'd visited one as a teenager and remember being unprepared for the pull of the undertow, even in a man-made wave pool. A small child still in diapers stood in front of me, a beautiful child who had me mesmerized. He had his feet in the surf of this wave pool, his back to the waves. Suddenly he was knocked over by a shove of water and pulled under. I was stunned, thinking, *I should do something, I should do something,* when his mother appeared, running into the water, grabbing him and lifting him out.

I told my father I regretted not acting quicker. I was

closer to the boy. I should have done something. I stared down at my feet, paused and then gave up a secret.

Dad, when I die, I really want to be a guardian angel. I want to watch over children and be an angel.

Dad stopped walking, looked at me for a moment, tilting his head as he always did when he searched for the right words. And then he said to me, "You know, I don't think they give you that job in Heaven unless you've done it on Earth first."

We didn't stay long at the beach. It was cold and still ahead, a three-hour drive back. When we finally made it back to Washington, Dad said he needed to gas up the car before he could return it to the rental place. He was driving through some neighborhoods I'd never seen, where windows had bars and walls had graffiti. He pulled into a gas station where the attendant sat behind bullet proof glass. I was scared.

Dad you can't stop here.

"Why not?"

It's dangerous. It's a bad neighborhood.

Dad ignored me. He parked and got out to get gas. I noticed a man lurking nearby. He was black. He had a ragged sweatshirt on and sweat pants. He looked dirty. I was scared of him.

Dad finished filling the car and walked over to the window to pay. The man walked up to our car. I was terrified. Did he have a gun? Would he carjack the car with me in it?

The man pulled out a rag and a spray bottle and started cleaning the windshield. Why was he doing this? Did he work for the gas station? I didn't think so.

Dad came back to the car and opened the door and leaned in. I was frantic.

Dad! Dad, what's he doing?!
"I think he wants a quarter."
Really?
Dad reached into the change dish and got a quarter. He gave it to the man, and the man smiled.

Chapter Twenty-One

"*W*hat are you going to call it?"

Call what?

"Your foundation."

It's not a foundation. It's a charitable donor fund.

"Whatever. What are you going to call it?"

Laura is my best female friend, a lifelong newspaper woman like me. She has a way of asking pointed questions, pressing someone to get to the point even if that person doesn't yet see the point.

We were working our way through a basket of chips and salsa at one of our favorite Mexican haunts. It was December 2003, and I'd been filling her in about my anonymous activities, the donations I was starting to make. To the food bank, the children's home, the addiction recovery center, the homeless shelter, the domestic violence shelter, the health clinic for illegal immigrants.

She'd seen the joy on my face as I described how Aunt Dorothy's money was now going to buy clothes and food and books for poor children, Christmas presents for kids in foster care, and basic necessities for teens over 18 who were no longer the responsibility of their parents, but unable because of addiction or dysfunction to care for themselves.

Laura had seen me through the worst of life. My divorce, the death of my parents, my breakdown. Now she was seeing me happy.

In her question, I felt the gentle push to move forward, to believe in what I was doing and give it a name.

AngelWorks.

"Angel Works?"

No. AngelWorks. All one word, but with the 'W' capitalized.

She smiled. Clearly I had already given this some thought.

I don't remember how the name AngelWorks came into my head; it seemed as if it had always been there.

I explained, studying her face for a reaction, that I had always wanted to be a guardian angel.

I didn't have to tell her.

I could see from her expression, she already knew.

Chapter Twenty-Two

*I*t was late December now, and Simon had returned. Simon was a cat, a black and white stray. He belonged to himself, but he shared himself with the neighborhood.

In the warmer months, Simon preferred to wander outside. I set food and water out for him; I left the garage door open a crack to provide him shelter. In the winter, when the temperature dipped below freezing, or in the spring, after an especially nasty thunderstorm, he would appear, often waiting on my porch chair until I opened the door.

I invited him inside. At first my other cats didn't like this; they would hiss at Simon who never retreated from a challenge. The fights would leave tufts of fur throughout the house. I trained the cats to get along by serving deli turkey to all of them as soon as Simon entered the house. Eventually Simon was granted entrée by the others; he came to sleep on my bed at night.

From the moment I first looked into Simon's eyes, I knew he was in my life for a purpose.

He'd first appeared shortly after my father died. He projected a wisdom, strength and confidence that reminded me of my father, the kind Dad had shown that day at the Washington D.C. gas station and countless other times. He was uncannily smart, too, always pausing to look both ways before crossing a street.

I thought myself silly to even think it, but I wondered if this cat carried a part of my father's soul. He seemed to be looking out for me, even as I was looking after him.

Neighborhood kids dashed my reincarnation theory when they told me the stray had been in the neighborhood for years. His name was "Stinky," they said.

Stinky?! That's no name for a cat!

I insisted the cat be called Simon. I gave him a name and food and shelter and shots. He gave me comfort.

And a story.

After I met Simon, I wrote "Santa's Stray," a children's story about a black and white stray cat who sneaks into a house where the garage door is left open on Christmas Eve. In the story, the cat — also named Simon — meets Santa Claus. The stray fears Santa will think he smells and throw him out of the house. But that is not Santa's way. Santa sees this cat has knowing eyes and learns that the cat loves children as much as Santa, and maybe even knows them better. In this way, so the story goes, Simon holds the secret to granting Santa's own Christmas wish: to know not just what the children want for Christmas, or whether they are good or bad, but whether they are happy and healthy or lonely and sad.

I read "Santa's Stray" to Henry's preschool class, then printed out copies and bound them to keep. It was a story about the value of all strays who want to belong and to give. I wanted to share it with everyone, but I didn't know how.

The story needed illustrations, a publisher.

Though I had no idea how to make it happen, I could imagine the book being sold to raise money for the homeless and the hungry, the strays of society. The idea would tease me at odd moments and I would tell Simon, *You're going to be famous someday!* I approached artists, the few I encountered, and asked if they were interested in such a project.

Two years went by before I found Carlene.

Carlene understood big dreams. Her eyes glistened like stars whenever she talked about her own: Since the time she was a child, she wanted to illustrate picture books. Carlene had a degree in illustration.

A mutual acquaintance put us together. I showed her the story. We met several times to discuss the book and how best to illustrate it, what medium, which images.

Carlene asked if it mattered what the cat looked like.

Oh yes! It has to look like the real Simon.

In December, after Simon was back, Carlene came to my house with a camera to take pictures. From those pictures would come rough sketches, then paintings.

I had no idea how to publish or sell a children's book, but somehow it didn't matter because now I had Carlene and I had AngelWorks.

Simon, you're going to be famous!

Chapter Twenty-Three

*W*ith the arrival of January 2004, I made a resolution to find meaning in life: I would try to become a better Mom, a better niece, but mostly, a better self.

Like so many women, I had spent too many years giving myself the lowest priority, so much so that I sometimes found only responsibility binding me to this life, but not desire.

I wanted to change that. I didn't yet know how. But I knew that I wanted to write and I wanted to help people.

The deaths that had stolen my parents had also provided me the financial ability to chase these dreams. All I lacked was the inner strength. I was still shaken from leaving my job. Anxieties still spun my head.

For this reason, I was avoiding Dorothy.

I had come to deeply love and respect her. I marveled at the intelligence that sustained her independence for so long. But since the last episode — was it a stroke? — she was declining. She grew agitated and paranoid. She started cleaning her apartment, sorting things, moving them, then removing them again. Purposeless activity it is called, I learned later. It's a sign of dying.

She began cutting her clothes. She cut the sleeves off shirts, the hems off pants. She cut flower arrangements apart.

Tommie was patient. She kept coming day after to day to visit Dorothy, to help Dorothy move the pictures on the walls, then move them back again.

I couldn't stand to watch. My visits grew brief, infrequent.

In mid-January, I found a message on my voice mail. It was Tommie. She said Dorothy wanted me to come see her. It was late in the day, after Tommie's shift had ended. I decided to go the next day because I could not bear to be alone with Dorothy when she was like this.

The next morning, I was on my way to Dorothy's when my cell phone rang. The caller ID said it was Tommie; I answered and immediately started talking.

Hi Tommie. Tell Dorothy I am in the car and on my way.

"Polly, Dorothy has collapsed," Tommie interrupted, her voice unsteady.

I felt myself stop breathing as I waited for the rest.

"I opened the door to the apartment and I just found her on the floor by the refrigerator. It looks like she hit her head on the way down. There's a dent in the fridge door. ..."

Tommie said the ambulance was already on its way.

I'll be right there.

Dorothy's apartment was full of people when I arrived: Tommie, the assisted-living nurses, the paramedics. I stepped through the open door, looked to my right and saw the dent in the fridge. Dorothy always was hard-headed and there's the proof, I thought.

I found Dorothy looking dazed, sitting on her bed while the paramedics held onto her so she wouldn't topple over. There were asking her if she knew what happened.

"I don't know," she said. "I don't know."

The nurses said she didn't seem to recognize anyone.

She recognized me.

The paramedics said she had a high fever and a rapid pulse. They wanted to take her the emergency room, but Dorothy wasn't cooperating.

I'd rarely told Dorothy what to do. At first I thought I was showing respect for her independence, but I think I feared the responsibility of making a decision for her. So many times I'd look over my shoulder for the older and wiser person who could tell me what to do.

But this time, there was no hesitation. I looked Dorothy in the eye.

Dorothy, you have to go with them.

She shook her head no.

Yes, Dorothy. You have to go with them. You are not well.

"I'm not?"

Dorothy, you have to go with them. Trust me. Do you trust me?

She looked at me.

"Okay."

The paramedics loaded her onto a gurney and headed for the hospital.

I arrived at the emergency room before the ambulance did.

I waited, surrounded by the beeping machines and fluorescent lights and smell of floor sanitizer.

Finally she arrived.

She was not conscious. The paramedics said she'd had a seizure. She was rolled into an ER holding room and hooked up to machines that monitored her oxygen saturation levels, her breathing rate, her pulse, her blood pressure.

Her pulse was high and her saturations were low, but

she appeared stable so the ER staff left us alone. Dorothy stirred somewhat and started talking.

But she wasn't talking to me.

She stared about six feet into the air above her.

"Okay, okay," she said, nodding, as though she were listening to someone I couldn't see.

Then she faded again, eyes half shut in a droop.

A computer monitor in the room caught my eye. A single word was blinking on the screen. I presumed it was the word that appeared whenever the computer was signed-off, but it startled me, leaving me transfixed.

Blinking at me was the word, "GOOD-BYE."

Time passed. I was in a daze as medical people came in and out of the room drawing blood for her, doing tests. We were alone when Dorothy suddenly stared shaking, violently, all over. My eyes darted to the monitor: Her pulse was spiking.

I ran for the ER doctor.

Medical people raced to the room and gave her a shot to stop the seizure. But even with that, it seemed to last an awfully long time. Her oxygen sats were falling rapidly so they put a mask on her. She reached to tug it off, but she was weak.

Hours passed as we sat there together, Dorothy dazed and trying to remove the oxygen mask. Me, replacing it gently, wondering if the mask was uncomfortable or if Dorothy was ready to die.

Tommie came and sat with her a while. I went back to Dorothy's apartment to get her purse and papers. I looked around, wondering if she would ever be back here. I made arrangements for my son's care and returned to Dorothy's bedside.

So many times in the hospital watching people die. I wondered if she would die first or if I would.

I finally went home to bed, wondering if I would get the call that would wake me and bring me back.

No call came. When I returned in the morning I found her assigned to a room. On the door was a sign that said, "DNR," indicating her Do Not Resuscitate order. Dorothy was essentially unchanged, but the nursing staff was complaining that she was fighting the oxygen mask. We marveled at how a woman could be so physically strong yet so ill at the same time.

What did it mean? Did it mean she wanted to die? Or did it mean she was still healthy and would recover?

I finally relented to a nurse's request to tie Dorothy's arms to the bed with restraints so she couldn't remove the mask. She hated the restraints and would fight them with all her lessening strength, leaning forward, her head dropping.

She resembled Christ hanging from the cross, and I felt like Judas.

The hours disappeared and I don't even remember leaving the hospital, but I remember waking to a phone call from the duty nurse. She said Dorothy was in tears, fighting the restraints. She felt it was a violation to keep them on. Would I give permission to remove them?

Yes, of course...

I didn't know how long it would take Dorothy to die if she took off her oxygen mask, but I knew that saturation levels below 90 percent were dangerous and Dorothy's had been dipping into the low 80s. I wondered if she would still be alive when I reached the hospital.

Dorothy was still alive, and the nurses were still struggling with her. Meanwhile, no doctor could give me a straight answer about her condition. What caused her collapse? Would she recover? Or was she dying?

I began to wonder whether she was ready for hospice. I read what literature I could find in the hospital on hospice and the stages of dying. It seemed to me that Dorothy was dying.

So I asked her doctor to come see me. The doctor, who had no answers to my other questions, easily answered this one.

"Yes, Dorothy clearly has enough symptoms to qualify for hospice care if that's the route you want to take."

Yes, please!

The doctor wrote the order for Dorothy to be evaluated for hospice the next day. I felt a measure of relief.

It wouldn't last.

The phone rang at 5 a.m. the next morning, January 19. The nurses said that Dorothy's oxygen saturation levels were dropping into the 60s and it appeared that death was imminent.

Tell her to wait for me.

I jumped out of bed, threw on clothes and raced through the cold, dark early morning toward the hospital. I found a beautiful sight when I arrived. Dorothy was surrounded by three nurses who were filling the room with their warmth and laughter. I was so grateful.

But with me finally there, the nurses left so Dorothy and I could be alone. The room was dark but for a bedside lamp. I knelt down at her side and grasped her hand, pressed my cheek to it and thanked her for coming into my life when I needed family most, when I needed someone to believe in me so I could grow and stop looking over my shoulder for someone older and wise.

And then Dorothy spoke.

"Look, look who's here."

I lifted my head, looked first at Dorothy and saw that she was smiling and pointing toward the foot of her bed.

Who is it Dorothy? Who do you see?

"Well can't you see? Don't you recognize him?"

I stared transfixed at the foot of the bed, longing with all my heart to see my father. And knowing somehow that was a privilege reserved for those about to die.

When I looked back at Dorothy, she was looking at me.

"I was wrong. I never wanted it."

What Dorothy?

"The money. I thought I wanted it. But I didn't really."

I placed my cheek against her hand again, telling her not to worry, that there was a fund now, and her money was going to do a lot of good.

Don't worry Dorothy. I love you!

Chapter Twenty-Four

*D*orothy didn't die. Not at that moment.

Instead, she became agitated. She tried to get out of bed but she was too weak.

"I want to go home, I want to go home." She looked at me in anger when I wouldn't help her get up.

I was startled. I went to look for the nurses. Up and down the hallways and no one to be found. It was 7 a.m. now, and the shifts were changing over. I saw a nurse's aide and begged her to come help me. She said she would come when she could.

I went back into Dorothy's room. She was naked, her hospital gown still entangled in her arms but no longer covering her drooping breasts.

I raced out of the room again, looking for someone to help me. I went to the nurses' station and begged for someone to come. They agreed to page Dorothy's nurse, but she didn't come.

I went back to Dorothy's room, and she was still naked, trying to get out of bed. The nurse's aide came by and eased Dorothy back into her gown. She placed the restraints back on Dorothy's arms, to keep her dressed and in bed.

Dorothy was angry. She fought and fought the restraints, hanging half slumped over. I tried to soothe her, but she would have none of it.

"Get out!" she shouted at me.

I dissolved into tears and went down to the cafeteria to get a cup of coffee. I sobbed uncontrollably in my booth. People walked by. I thought someone would say something to me, but no one did.

I collected myself and headed back upstairs to Dorothy's room. I saw two doctors by the nursing station and lashed out at them.

What does it take to get a nurse to the bedside of a dying woman in this hospital?!

The doctors asked the manager of the nursing station to page the nurse again.

When I got to Dorothy's room, the new nurse on duty was there.

She lashed out at me: "I've been in here. Where have YOU been for the last 20 minutes?"

The nurse explained that the floor was short on staff, and my great aunt, was, after all, a DNR. She had to put the priority on patients whose lives the hospital was trying to save.

About that time, a lab technician entered the room. She tried to take Dorothy's blood for another test. Dorothy started fighting. The lab tech called for someone to help her hold Dorothy down so she could force her to give blood.

What are you doing?! She doesn't need that. She's dying.

"Sorry, doctor's orders. We have to."

No! I am her health care power of attorney. No!

The nurse came in to mediate.

Why are they doing this when she's being transferred to hospice today?

"There's no order for hospice in her chart," the nurse said.

What do you mean there's no order for hospice in her chart? I discussed it with the doctor yesterday.

"There's no order in her chart," the nurse insisted.

I took the chart from her, started flipping backward through pages and found the order.

SEE?! It's right there!

"Well it's not in her orders for today."

WHAT?! Call the doctor. Call the doctor now!

The nurse went out in the hall and came back and handed me the phone. It was the doctor. She explained that the order for hospice had been cancelled earlier when the nurses on the previous shift thought Dorothy's death was imminent.

So reinstate the order.

The doctor said she would, but since it was already mid-morning she didn't know whether hospice would be able to come out and do the evaluation today. Dorothy couldn't be transferred to the hospice facility until she was evaluated.

I looked at Dorothy. I didn't know who was going to die first: Dorothy, or me from the stress, or these hospital people from justifiable homicide.

I wanted to call hospice myself, but my cell phone battery was dead. So I went to my car and plugged it into the charger. I didn't know the number so I called information for Harry Hynes Memorial Hospice. The number information gave me was wrong. I threw the phone against the dashboard and started screaming. It was a nightmare. I needed help, but I couldn't get anyone to help me.

Okay, deep breath.

I called information again and asked if they had a different number. They had three. I called the hospice in-patient unit first and a nice woman with a gentle voice said, sorry, but we don't schedule evaluations.

I was about to cry again.

Then I remembered Nadine.

Nadine was a grief counselor at Harry Hynes hospice I had met with once for help dealing with the death of my parents. I got her voice mail. I left a long desperate rambling message full of pain, begging for someone to please, please get my Aunt Dorothy out of this hospital.

She needs help to die. And I need help, too!

I was headed back upstairs to see Dorothy when my cell phone rang. It was another woman from Harry Hynes'. She said she'd heard from Nadine, and had already spoken with Dorothy's doctor to confirm the order for transfer. She told me not to worry, that she would be up to evaluate Dorothy at 1 p.m. and we could arrange transfer after that.

By 1 p.m. Dorothy's sats had dipped into the 60s again. Her breathing was labored. I wondered if she was suffocating. I tried to place the oxygen mask on her but again she took it off.

The evaluation was quick. Dorothy was clearly dying. The ambulance was ordered to come pick her up. It was the same crew that had brought her into the ER just four days earlier, when I'd had to tell Dorothy to trust me and go with them.

The crew warned me that some hospice patients don't survive the trip. Did I understand?

Yes.

Dorothy didn't look like Dorothy anymore as she was loaded onto the gurney, wrapped in blankets to protect against the January cold. Her stare was vacant, her cheeks sunken, her skin, a strange cast.

I followed the ambulance as it made its way four miles across town to the in-patient hospice facility. The minute I arrived, I felt relief. I was escorted to a warmly inviting suite with a home-like bedroom and adjacent sitting area with a sofa and coffee table.

Dorothy was brought in and made comfortable. No more restraints. No more struggle. The nurse examined her and said it would be soon. Her level of skin mottling indicated that her heart and lungs were failing.

I sat next to Dorothy and stared at her, holding her hand.

A woman came in with a dinner tray. I looked at her, confused. Surely she knew my great aunt was beyond being able to eat.

"No, it's for you."

I'm not hungry.

"She would want you to eat."

I considered this and realized I hadn't eaten all day.

Okay. I'll eat.

She set the tray down on the coffee table by the sofa, and gestured toward the dessert cart outside in the hall. I went over and picked out a slice of cherry pie.

Then I sat down on the sofa, took a bite of tuna fish sandwich and looked up.

Oh!

She was dead.

Dorothy died and I missed it. I called the nurse to make sure. She came and checked and said yes, she's gone. Then the nurse turned and left, closing the door behind her.

You did it Dorothy, you did it!
I was cheering her.

You made it, you made it, you made it!

I turned and looked away from her face, to a space six feet above here where she'd stared in the ER room. I wondered if her soul was now hovering over me.

Was she in the arms of angels?

Was I?

I scattered rose petals from a bedside flower over her body. And then I sat down to eat the pie.

Chapter Twenty-Five

"*W*hat To Do When Someone Dies: A Checklist."
I'd torn the article out of a magazine months before.
Now I carried it with me, along with my own list of things
I needed to do and people I needed to see:

Funeral home.
Obituary.
Lawyer.
CPA.
Financial advisor.
Retirement home.
Moving company.
Storage unit.
Estate sales person.

I headed to the funeral home with the same enthusiasm
of a cat leaping into a bathtub.

Thanks to the wonders of the Internet, I had chosen
the funeral home long before Dorothy died, taking care to
find someone reputable who did cremation. When I asked
Dorothy what she wanted done with her remains she had
grimaced and said, "Just throw me on the ground."
I'd decided to scatter ashes in the same cemetery where
my grandmother — Dorothy's eldest sister — was buried
alongside her other sister, her parents and my father.

I told the funeral director no, I didn't need a funeral

because really there was only myself and my son Henry. He took me to his showroom of crematory urns. I teased him, showing off my extensive knowledge of crematory vessels.

Now I don't want one of those boxes you can't open. My brother had to use a hacksaw to get my father's open. Don't you have a simple scattering box? Something artsy-craftsy like we got for Mom?

He showed me a plastic box that opened easily with a screw driver. I could have that for $25. I figured Dorothy, the woman who'd salvaged her husband's casket, would like that.

He gave me a form to fill out for the obituary. I objected.

Couldn't I just write it myself? I wrote my father's and my mom's. I'd really prefer to write it myself.

I could see I was appearing difficult. I poked fun and tried to lighten the mood. Mine, if not his.

Do you have a closet full of black suits like that?

He said yes, but the one he was wearing was the only one that still fit. I was relieved; he was capable of humor. I had been through too much grief to be treated by the book. I needed a little human connection here.

For reasons I do not remember, he told me his dog had recently died. He said he missed the dog lying at his feet after work. He said his mother really felt he should get another dog.

Your mother is still alive?

I was surprised because he looked at least 20 years older than me, and my mother was dead, after all.

Yes, he said. His mother was still alive and still mothering him.

Well, I am a mother of a son, too. And I say, by all means, listen to your mother. Get another dog.

Somewhere there is a dog that needs you.

I called the lawyer. He said there wasn't much he could do until we received the death certificates.

Death certificates! I left that off my list!

He told me to get the names, addresses and Social Security numbers of the prospective heirs and he would prepare the filings. My great aunt had died without a will, "in testate," so we would need to petition the probate court to name me administrator and to present the names of those we believed to be heirs under state law.

My Uncle Turley was Dorothy's closest living relative. He was 82 and her nephew. He had voluntarily withdrawn himself from inheritance, but I had since persuaded him to place himself back in the line of heirs. He would get a third of her estate.

The other two thirds would go to the children of Dorothy's other niece and nephew. That included my father and my aunt, who were both dead. All this meant ultimately I would get a ninth of my aunt's estate.

Before she died, I had transferred another $100,000 to the charitable fund, so this meant there was roughly a million left.

I visited Steve, the financial planner. He quickly started punching numbers on a calculator, figuring how much I would get for my share plus administrator expenses.

Dorothy hadn't yet been dead 24 hours.

It seems a bit soon to be thinking about that. I don't want to think about that now.

I called the CPA. He said he couldn't do much either without death certificates, but he said to take note of the values of her stocks on the date of death. That would become the basis for inheritance taxes.

Already done.

He also told me to apply for a new Social Security number for her estate.

You need that?

I didn't know.

I swung over to the retirement home to gather up her valuables, including a cardboard box she'd told me contained the ashes of her late husband; Milton was in the closet. I made arrangements to immediately vacate the apartment. Her belongings would go to a storage unit. An estate sales company could liquidate them. The nursing staff hugged me and traded stories about the independent woman we'd all come to love. They asked me when Dorothy's services would be. Several people at the home had been asking.

Oh?

I told them I had not planned on a funeral, that I was sick of grieving rituals. I could see the disappointment on their faces. I quickly reversed my decision.

Perhaps we could do something here. In a couple of days, in the afternoon after my son gets out of school?

They liked that. It was agreed. They would spread the word.

I took the box with Uncle Milton's ashes home and placed it the garage, wrote Dorothy's obituary, and then added to my list:

Florist.

Chocolates.

Guest registry.

Memorial folders.

Eulogy.

I don't know why I decided to do it all myself. As much as I was sick of grief rituals, I understood there were others who needed to grieve Dorothy, and I couldn't deny them; it was important. My son Henry, especially, was relieved.

At the service I invited everyone to share a memory. Henry said he loved his Aunt Dorothy, that she enjoyed watching him jump and spin and always liked his kisses.

I told a story about how my aunt preferred my long hair when I wore it up and out of my face, and how someone had said I should wear it up at the service in her honor.

I am wearing it down in her honor, instead. Because more than any other trait in a woman, Dorothy valued independence.

Chapter Twenty-Six

I stared down from the airplane window at the Bahaman Islands.

They were covered with scrubby brush, not the palm trees I expected. Turquoise waters traced the shoreline, in curvaceous patterns formed by shallows of the sand.

Nothing about it seemed real.

It was late January. Winter storms were moving in at home. Aunt Dorothy had died less than a week before. I'd retrieved her ashes from the funeral home only days before.

And now I was in paradise.

So why did I want to die?

My sister and I had planned the trip months before, lured by an ad in a travel magazine promising pristine white sand beaches. The Four Seasons, Grand Exuma Island.

Peggy had dropped the ad down toward me while I was visiting her the previous Thanksgiving. I watched it sail down from a view-out railing on the upper floor of her home, floating back and forth unpredictably. I caught it with both hands.

Yes!

I knew immediately I wanted to go. I'd never been to a tropical beach but I felt a longing for the beach, even before I saw the sea with my father for the first time. Something about the beach felt safe to me, so much so that when my therapist asked me to visualize a safe place, I always ended up on a beach. I saw myself alone, surrounded by warm sand and cool breezes.

She asked me, Why a beach? I couldn't explain. But I remembered that during my teen years I had a wall-size mural of a palm tree-lined beach in my bedroom. The beach was my escape even then.

A chauffer met us at the airport and escorted us to a black stretch limousine.

A limo?

My sister explained that she'd hired the limo so we could travel to the resort in style. I'd never been in a limo before. All I knew about the interior of a limo was what I'd seen in movies.

Do people really have sex in here?

I fought back the feeling of unreality as I tried to make sense of what I was doing in a limo. Curiosity gave way to guilt as we drove past the local communities on the way to the resort. Run-down buildings lined the street. Everything looked old and dirty. Like images of Haiti I'd seen on TV. So strange, these poor communities, side by side with the posh resorts.

It didn't make sense.

Nothing seemed to make sense any more.

Once at the resort, we were checked into our room. I asked the bell hop how to get to the ocean and he pointed past the bed, to a set of plantation doors.

"That way."

He opened the doors and I was stunned. The beach was right there. Sand at our back patio doorstep. Turquoise shallows, leading to ocean, just a hundred yards away.

If Dorothy's dying hours were the most horrible thing I had ever witnessed, this was now the most beautiful. The contrasting extremes left me numb.

In the hospital, as she lay dying, and in the days that followed as I made plans to empty her apartment and plan her funeral, it seemed there was no one to help me.

Now I lounged by a pool overlooking an ocean as cabana boys supplied me with fresh towels and banana daiquiris. In the restaurant I would dine on lobster pizza. In the spa, women from Bali would scrub, wrap and wash my naked body. During the day I would learn to snorkel and pluck conch shells from the shallows. At night I would stare up from the Jacuzzi at the stars.

The resort was warm, beautiful and safe.

But I found myself wanting to die.

I walked out toward the tide in the darkness one night, a darkness punctured only by the light of stars and powerful sound of the sea. I imagined walking into the water, letting the tide swallow me unto death. My heart felt so heavy I would surely sink into the darkness.

I was already sinking under the weight of grief over Dorothy, over resurgent grief over Mom and Dad. Why was I left here alone and alive?

Please give me permission to die.

Who was I asking? My family? Myself? God?

I could imaging them all saying, "No, you need to live. Even if you don't want to right now, you need to."

But if I hurt this much in paradise, how do I go on at home?

There was no answer.

I looked back toward the shore, toward the lights of the

resort and thought of Henry, my son. He would always be my light in the darkness.

I could never leave him.

Never.

I turned and walked away from the tide.

Chapter Twenty-Seven

I *won't be idled with despair.*

Over and over I kept telling myself this, even as dark moods pulled me toward the bed. I knew who I wanted to be, and she wasn't depressed. She was a strong woman, an energetic mother, an optimistic friend, someone who would make better the lives of those around her.

And so I fought back.

I sought a life of meaning.

What would a life of meaning look like? I didn't yet know. What did I want out of life? I made a list of Wildest Dreams.

Publish book

Take Henry to see volcanoes in Hawaii

Get back to a size 8

Grow a healthy garden

It was a start. Wishing is always a good place to start, I'd decided.

Settling Dorothy's estate was more waiting game than work. I had done most of the work already when I consolidated her assets. There were still old tax returns to file, but the CPA had that well in hand. Now it was mostly a matter of filing documents with the court and waiting for unknown potential heirs to come forward. I knew there were none, so I didn't worry. The money, we already knew, would be divided between my grandmother's offspring — my Uncle Turley, myself, my brother and sister, and two cousins. My sister asked if an early partial distribution was possible; the judge authorized it.

With another windfall coming to me out of nowhere, I started looking around my home. The landscaping was terrible. A greenhouse built off the lower level was in disrepair, an eyesore and a source of draft. I sought bids for a new greenhouse. I called a landscape architect.

And I recalled a conversation years earlier with my Dad, on my theory of why some people obsess over fixing up their houses: *They can't make their lives perfect so they try to make their houses perfect.* Dad thought it a good theory.

I was guilty of this and I knew it, but fixing up my house and yard felt like doing something positive. Thanks to Dorothy, I could easily afford it.

When the salesman from the sunroom company came to my house, I asked whether the poor economy was hurting business. He said no, their clientele seem to be insulated from the swings that were causing local job loss.

"Affluent people like yourself seem to do a good job of managing their money," he said.

I looked at him, annoyed.

"Oh, I'm not a good money manager. I've just had a lot of people in my life die."

The landscape architect met with me and asked what I wanted.

That was easy: A big vegetable garden. Lilac bushes, forsythia, hyacinth, hydrangea, roses.

"Grandma's garden?" she asked.

Yes!

I wanted my yard filled with the flowers of my childhood, the ones from the farm in Oklahoma, the ones from my childhood home. I couldn't bring the people back, but I could have the flowers. Maybe in the flowers, those I'd lost could bloom again.

I finalized plans for the greenhouse and the landscaping and waited for the change, wondering if it would be as good as I hoped.

Chapter Twenty-Eight

*A*ngelWorks got off to a slow start. With Dorothy's death — and the ensuing estate matters — I lost momentum. But somehow, the ideas for helping people kept coming. They would be there in my mind, in the early morning hours, as I awakened. And they would not let go.

I started chasing several ideas at once, hoping that eventually one would be a success. These included:

A book about Simon called "Santa's Stray," which I hoped to use to raise money for the hungry.

A free, online database that could match would-be volunteers with charities, churches and schools in need of people with specific skills.

A scholarship program to provide low-income, gifted kids with paid memberships to the local science museum.

A grant program to help teen-agers design and carry out their own solutions to community problems.

A memorial for miscarried and still-born children.

It surprised me how hard it was to give money away.

I wrote letters and proposals, addressed boards of directors, attended meeting after meeting. I started "going to lunch," by which I mean I started schmoozing. As a journalist, I'd shunned schmoozing for fear it would taint me. Ethical journalists, after all, were not supposed to take more than a cup of coffee from a source, much less buy each other lunch. That could create a conflict of interest.

I found I had to sell both myself and my ideas; the pledge of money was not enough. Skeptics asked who I was, what was in it for me and why had they never heard of me before?

I prepared written statements answering these questions, explaining that I was a career journalist who came into control of family money that was now being put toward charity. I explained there was nothing in it for me, except to make a difference in my community.

I waited out one board for more than six months; to my astonishment, the group met only one hour a month and kept tabling a decision on my proposal.

Frustrating as it was, I realized I was learning a lot. Learning more than I had in a long time.

The scholarship program at the local science museum was the first to take off. AngelWorks offered to pay the annual membership for up to 100 children who were both academically gifted and whose family income qualified them for free or reduced-price school lunches.

The idea came from watching my son. From the time it first opened, Exploration Place was Henry's favorite place to go. Visits to the exhibits ignited fascinations with human biology and space. I was heartsick when I discovered Henry had classmates who were as bright and insatiably curious as him, but who rarely visited the museum because of the cost.

Just how many low-income, gifted students were there? The school district estimated about 400. I thought of my father, growing up poor in a single parent family, unable to afford college if not for World War II and the G.I. Bill that paid his way. What would the world have lost if his curiosity had not been given opportunity to flourish?

The museum and school district agreed on terms for the program and an application went out. To qualify, I asked only that students write a single page in their own hand, describing why they wanted membership to the museum.

As the deadline neared, I wondered if anyone would apply. Two days before the deadline, only a handful of applications were turned in. Then the deadline came. More than 40 kids between the ages of 5 and 13 responded.

Their words moved me. Within these children was everything I had expected to find and wanted to help:

> *"My name is Sam and I am 8 years old, and ever since I was 5 I wanted to be a scientist..."*

> *"I have only been to Exploration Place two times. I want to learn all about the human body."*

> *"If I get picked to be an Explore Kid I would be so proud of myself, and so would my parents..."*

> *"I am 9 years old and always wanting to know how and why things do the way they do. I have always wanted to come down to Exploration Place, but money is tight. My Mom is laid off..."*

> *"I don't go to Exploration Place often, and I would have more friends if I did go."*

Applicants were told that winners would be invited to a special pizza party in their honor. Several of the kids mentioned the pizza. The comments were revealing:

"If you choose me can you save a slice for my sister?"

*"Can I have two extra slices so I can give
one to my sister and one to my Mom?"*

Clearly, these were kids for whom pizza was a rare treat, not a basic food group as in my household.

Judy, the development director for the museum, gave me a binder full of the children's essays to take home and read. Page after page of essays on lined notebook paper written in pencil. Young children describing big dreams. Each one an eager learner full of curiosity and ambition. And each one from a home that was poor.

I hugged the binder to my chest and smiled.

Tears welled up in my eyes.

Time and again, I had asked myself, *Why am I here in this life?*

To raise my son, of course.

But I also longed for a deeper sense of purpose. And now I knew.

This is why.

To help them.

And others like them.

Chapter Twenty-Nine

*L*ike nearly all of my ideas, the idea for Mother's Day was simply there in my mind as I awoke one morning.

Mother's Day is such a sad day for so many of us: for those whose mothers have died, for mothers whose children have died, and for women unable to have children at all.

It was pain my mother had felt through nearly a decade spent unable to conceive. It was pain I'd felt myself through my own years of infertility, a miscarriage, and since the death of my mother.

I wanted to spare others that hurt. Or at least ease their pain a bit.

How?

With flowers – acres and acres of flowers.

What if Botanica could be open free to the public on Mother's Day?

Botanica, Wichita's botanical gardens, were at their most beautiful in May, with blooming peonies bending under the weight of their full blossoms and tea roses exploding with color.

When Mom was alive I'd taken her on Mother's Day, our last one together, and she'd marveled at the sight. And after she died, I had a brick with her name placed in a garden walkway.

Admission was usually $6 an adult, $3 for kids 5 and

older, or $12 per family. A fair price, but too expensive for many of our local families, I knew.

What if it were free?

What if we could invite the public and pay special tribute to those who usually feel left out of Mother's Day?

What if we said, this day is for you to grieve your pain and honor your loss? What if we told them, today all these flowers of the garden are for you?

I called Botanica and asked for a meeting. I explained briefly what I wanted to do, and asked them, Could you tell me how many people came last year on Mother's Day? When admission was paid? Donna, the development director, said she would get the figure.

It was April, and Mother's Day was little more than a month away. If I was going to pull this off, I needed to avoid the obstacles I encountered before. So I'd arrived at the meeting ready with detailed information about myself, AngelWorks and my idea, as well as benefits to Botanica and the community.

To my surprise, the idea was immediately approved. Donna said Botanica had about 500 visitors the previous Mother's Day. We agreed that more people would surely come if admission was free.

So how much should AngelWorks pay for sponsorship?

I offered $18,000 with the understanding the free event be underwritten for the next three years.

The date was set: May 9 would be AngelWorks' first major event in the community.

Angie, Botanica's marketing whiz, went to work immediately, arranging advertising, news coverage and TV and radio appearances.

TV?! I have to do TV?! I'm a newspaper person. I can't do TV!

Angie just smiled and said I would be great.

How could I do the morning news show? I don't have anyone to watch Henry at that hour!

Angie just smiled and said she would be happy to come over and watch Henry while I went to the TV studio.

TV?! I don't have anything to wear! What do you wear on TV?

Angie just smiled.

And I went shopping.

When I walked into Talbot's, I spied a friendly clerk who looked about my age.

"Oh! I have the skirt that matches that," I said, pointing to the vest she was wearing.

"Then you bought it about 10 years ago," she said.

Hmm. Yes, she was right. I hadn't had much reason to shop at Talbot's since I'd left Washington; I was happy with jeans.

I confessed my fashion ignorance to the clerk.

How long are skirts supposed to be now?

Are blouses supposed to be worn in or out?

I told her I was going on TV.

Please help me not look too fat.

She brought me a brightly patterned mini skirt and a choice of linen jackets: Blue. Pink. Blue. Pink. I couldn't make up my mind. Yellow?

I settled on blue *and* yellow, glad for the variety when I ended up doing three separate TV appearances. Angie came and sat with Henry as they watched me do the morning news show live.

Being on TV was hard to get my head around. I watched

the video tape at home. Under my face were my name and the word "AngelWorks." It was there like AngelWorks was something real, not just something I did at home from my basement office.

When Mother's Day arrived, I wondered if anyone would come.

Henry and I arrived at the gardens early. We found the parking lot full; we double–parked in the employee lot. I took a seat by the entrance and watched the front doors.

People streamed in almost endlessly. Donna said they were lined up for an hour before opening time. Hundreds of people came up, then thousands. I watched them come in the doors, my mouth half open in shock. There were families with children, retirees with their elderly parents, people in wheelchairs with oxygen tanks, and the visibly poor and infirm.

I walked the grounds and saw them eating picnics together on the lawns, taking family photos in the gardens. Inside, the vending machines ran out of pop. The director hustled extra toilet papers to the bathrooms.

And still, the crowds kept coming. Where they were parking, I couldn't guess. Most showed up cheerful and happy; for others, the visit was poignant.

An elderly woman sought me out. She was pushing her own mother in a wheelchair. The pair hadn't visited the gardens in more than five years, she said, because they couldn't afford it.

"Thank you," she told me.

I hugged her and fought back tears.

You're welcome.

Still more people came up to say thanks, including a

number of women who said their children had died. I hugged them, too, as we cried.

I had suspected there were other hurting hearts out there, longing to find solace on Mother's Day, but I had no idea there were so many. I had no idea that given a chance to spend a day in the gardens so many would come if only it was free.

In the four hours Botanica was open that afternoon, nearly 5,000 people came. Never had the gardens seen so many people in an afternoon.

This is why, I thought to myself.

This is why.

Chapter Thirty

*T*he front door bell rang.

I ignored it.

It was around noon on Memorial Day and I was taking a nap. Henry was out of town with his Dad, due back late that afternoon. I was weary of people so I ignored the door.

There had been so many people this May. Workmen were at the house almost daily constructing the new sunroom. Landscapers had reshaped the lawn, building gardens where there had been none. It was beautiful, but I craved peace.

The success of the Mother's Day event at the gardens had drained me. Certainly I was thankful for the massive turnout, but for days leading up to the event I felt like the poster child for grief: Telling the story over and over of my mother's death. Meeting and comforting strangers whose pain I understood.

And here it was Memorial Day.

No day to escape grief.

Already this day I'd driven 20 miles to the rural cemetery to place a small flag where my Dad's ashes were buried next to his mother Marie, and her mother, Florence. Henry and I had scattered Dorothy's ashes here the previous Palm Sunday, leaving a sandy trail on the grass which traced a line from her mother's grave to her sister's and then her other sister's and then my Dad's.*

By Memorial Day, there was no more trace of Dorothy in the grass.

When I got home from the cemetery, I crawled into bed and went to sleep. And ignored the bell.

Hours later, it rang again.

I opened the door to find a neighbor standing there.

Though he lived only two houses away, I barely knew him. He'd come to my house before, to ask about Simon, the stray. He'd been feeding Simon, too. Now the neighbor's face was grim.

"I tried to find you earlier …"

I was unprepared for what was coming.

"Simon is dead."

I put my hand over my mouth.

"I found him at the end of my driveway this morning. I thought he was asleep. I tried to wake him so I could move my car. But he was dead."

He asked me if I wanted the cat's body.

Yes. Please.

The neighbor went to get Simon. And shaking, I went across the street. I found the other neighbor who also loved Simon.

Please help me bury him.

Both neighbors met me in the corner of my backyard, a recessed, wooded area under a giant cottonwood tree. One brought Simon in a cardboard box. The other brought a shovel. The two men took turns digging.

---

* I'd intended to also scatter the ashes of Dorothy's husband Milton, but I found him securely sealed in a brass jar. He remains uncorked in my garage.

I opened the box hoping it wouldn't really be Simon.

It was. Flies buzzed around his rigid body. I studied his face. His wise, gentle face. I couldn't see his beautiful blue eyes, but I knew they were there. I looked him over. He looked perfect, healthy, strong. But dead.

Oh Simon.

I knew a lot about death by now. I knew there was no point in bargaining with God to bring him back. No point in being angry, seeking someone to blame or denying it had happened. I had no energy for those emotions any more.

Oh Simon.

When the hole was dug, the neighbor who brought him to me asked me if I wanted to place Simon in the grave.

Yes, thank you.

I wondered if it would be dangerous to my health to touch a dead cat, but I did it anyway. His body was stiff. He'd become rigid in a side sleeping position, in a shape like a crescent moon.

I placed him into the shallow grave and began scooping dirt over him with my hands. I clawed at the dirt, my pain finally rising to the surface and tears streaming down my face. More and more dirt, until my nails were full of mud and I watched Simon's face disappear from sight.

One of the men stopped me, urged me to go inside. He said they would finish. I suddenly realized what I had been doing, collected myself and went inside to wait.

Finally the men came to the door. I hugged them both and thanked them. Here we were, three grown adults grief–stricken over a cat, and yet we all knew, there was something truly special about Simon.

A car pulled up in the driveway. It was my ex-husband bringing back Henry. I sat Henry down on the sofa and told him the news immediately. He started crying. His father and I took him in the backyard to see the grave.

I told Henry it was a terrible thing, yes, but that it seemed Simon had died peacefully. He wasn't run over or attacked by another animal, after all. He just died.

While Henry and I cried together, I found words I hoped would comfort him. I said Simon was a good cat and that I had to believe there was a place in Heaven for cats like him.

And you never know, Henry. God might decide to send another stray our way.

Less than 10 minutes later, a woman came to our door. "Is this one of yours?"

It was a small, emaciated calico cat. She looked pregnant.

No, I have never seen her before.

The little cat was clearly starving. I went to get a can of cat food and brought it to the porch. She devoured it and another half can within minutes.

As Henry and I watched her eat, we started to smile. We couldn't do anything about Simon, but this cat, we could help.

"I'm surprised how much better I feel," said Henry.

Me, too, Henry. Me, too.

Chapter Thirty-One

$\mathcal{S}$imon wasn't the only loved-one we lost on Memorial Day. That evening I learned my Uncle Ben also had died.

Ben married my father's sister during World War II. He was like my father in many ways — an engineer of quiet genius and quiet nobility. I had kept track of his condition since January; he'd fallen gravely ill about the same time Dorothy died.

I started trading regular emails with his sons, Jim and Ron, two cousins I'd hardly known for the simple reason they were 15-20 years older than me.

For years, our age difference seemed an impenetrable boundary. But now we had a great deal in common. We were adult orphans from the same family. My cousins were also unexpected heirs of Aunt Dorothy's fortune.

We e-mailed regularly, and in their stories about our shared heritage I felt as though I had discovered a real treasure. The age difference that had separated us now proved a tremendous blessing. Because they were so much older, they were full of first-hand stories about Grandma and Dad and Dorothy, stories I had never heard.

When I learned of Ben's death, I grieved for them. I knew what was ahead: The funeral, the estate details, the sorting through of a lifetime of their parents' belongings.

I drove to Oklahoma to meet them at the funeral chapel for the viewing. I took a deep breath and walked in to look at the body. Life had taught me by now that dead bodies never really look like the person you knew, so in a strange way, that made it easier.

I studied what was left of Ben.

Hello, Death. We meet again.

The funeral was the next day. I watched my cousin Jim deliver a eulogy that brought tears and laughter to all of us gathered. I remembered speaking at Mom's service, and how I couldn't bring myself to speak at Dad's. Such a hard thing, a child trying to sum up the meaning of a parent's life.

After the funeral and the family lunch and a final gathering at Ben's house, I headed back to the bed and breakfast where I'd booked a room.

The former oil mansion resembled a castle. The walls were covered with photos of wedding couples who'd married here. In my room, a journal full of hand-written accounts of couple's celebrating honeymoons and anniversaries.

I poured a glass of wine and started to write my own entry:

I didn't come here for a wedding. I came for a funeral...

I don't remember drinking more than one glass, but by the time I got ready for bed, I somehow managed to brush my teeth with sun block instead of toothpaste.

Yech!

I grabbed the sun block bottle and read the warning label. I panicked and called my sister to tell her what I'd done.

Am I going to die?!

She laughed.

"No, you're not going to die."

Are you sure? How do you know?

Are you sure I'm not going to die?

Chapter Thirty-Two

$\mathcal{S}$ummer finally arrived, Henry was off school, and I made it a priority to do nothing. Which is to say, I relented to Henry's requests for digital cable and replaced our old 13-inch television with a new, 27-inch, flat-screen model.

Together we made a study of superheroes.

We started with Superfriends, then worked our way through the first complete season of the 1970s Wonder Woman series, then all four Superman movies. In the midst of this, I went to Spiderman 2 at the movie theater four times, then rented Spiderman 1 on video and watched it twice.

I tried to make it educational.

What makes a hero? I asked Henry.

It was a question that always fascinated me.

As a child, I liked to dress up often as Wonder Woman, and sometimes as Bat Girl. I would go to sleep at night imagining myself flying down from the sky, cape waving, to right playground wrongs.

In my adult life, I reveled in the idea of journalist as superhero. I wanted to be Lois Lane, sidekick to Superman. On my desk at work, I kept a toy Daily Planet building with a tiny plastic Superman that spun around it.

What makes a hero?

It's not the superpowers, I tried to impress upon Henry.

It's the choices they make. It's how they use their powers — and what they do when they don't have their powers at all.

My favorite example of this is in Spiderman 2: Peter Parker has lost his Spiderman powers of extreme strength and agility. Yet when he encounters a child trapped in a burning building, he risks his life to enter the fire and rescue the child anyway. He does this because he can't <u>not</u> do it.

What makes a hero?

Using power to help others ahead of yourself — and then still helping others when you don't have any special power, when it doesn't come easily at all.

At least that's what I told Henry.

Chapter Thirty-Three

$\mathcal{I}$t is mid-summer and the Catholic Church wants to know where the money I am offering them comes from. They want to know before they will take it.

I am in final negotiations with the local soup kitchen, which is under the financial oversight of the Catholic Church, to accept a $20,000 grant for the purposes of publishing my children's book, "Santa's Stray," so its soup kitchen can raise money.

I have proposed that AngelWorks give the soup kitchen the money to publish 10,000 copies of the book, which they may then offer for suggested contributions of $10 each.

"It sounds too good to be true," Wendy said when I first presented the idea. She runs the soup kitchen known as The Lord's Diner. I told her she could keep all the money raised by the book, that I hoped we could raise $100,000.

Of course, I knew it would depend on whether anyone would want to buy my book about the stray cat who helps Santa Claus.

I thought the story was good. And I knew Carlene's oil paintings for the book were already coming out beautifully. I presented Wendy with a copy of the story and two of Carlene's illustrations and asked her to think about whether she wanted to do this.

Henry worried.

"Mom, what if they say no? I won't be able to stand it if they say no."

I told Henry not to feel that way; this was up to God.

Either it is going to happen or it isn't. I want to do this for God, not for myself.

Okay, that wasn't entirely true. Of course I wanted this for myself.

I was on guard against the feeling constantly. But I didn't want money.

I wanted to do something meaningful, to tell a story about what it is like to be a stray, to feel left out but to want to belong. To want to give and to serve, but to hold back for fear of being rejected. I wanted to tell my story through Simon.

I worried constantly that this was a selfish act of ego, using my great aunt's money to publish my own book. What if nobody bought the book? What if we wasted $20,000 that could simply have been used to feed the hungry instead of a book publishing venture?

I was prepared for a lot of questions — but not the one about the source of Dorothy's money.

Why do they want to know that?

Wendy explained that church officials didn't want to be embarrassed in case the local newspaper dug up some dirt on me and my money.

Oh jeez, again with the newspaper. Don't they know the people who dig up dirt at the paper used to work for me? They already know all about me.

I tried to douse my initial resentment. It was a fair question.

I sent Wendy the paperwork I had already prepared about who I was and explaining AngelWorks, along with a new statement explaining that my great aunt invested in nearly 30 stocks, many of which she held for more than 30 years.

But I couldn't contain myself. I dashed off an email:

I'm hardly a good Catholic girl. I am a divorced Presbyterian. Does that make me not good enough to feed the hungry?

Wendy didn't engage. She responded with a brief e-mail thanking me and saying she had what she needed and all would be fine. I was grateful she'd let it go.

We set a schedule to present the text and the finished oil paintings to the publisher by the end of August. The publisher, in turn, agreed to deliver 10,000 books by the first of October.

Everything was on track, except the church's lawyer still hadn't approved the contract allowing the soup kitchen to take the grant money.

The lawyer said the deal could conceivably threaten the soup kitchen's non-profit status if the IRS decided that I was using a donation to a charity to essentially invest in my own book with the idea of making money off the book later if it proved a success.

Oh, did that sting.

Yes, I had hoped all along that if "Santa's Stray" was a success, a commercial publisher would eventually pick it up for national distribution.

The answer was obvious: I would give the story copyright to the soup kitchen, surrendering any future financial claim to the story.

That satisfied the lawyer and it satisfied me.

I wanted to be the author of a successful children's book — but I didn't need to make money off it.

Chapter Thirty-Four

I'd always said I never wanted to be rich, but by August I sure felt like I was.

Aunt Dorothy's estate cleared probate and I was able to distribute nearly a million dollars to the family.

My share was more than $100,000. It was the third inheritance I'd received in less than two and a half years. It didn't add up to a fortune, mind you. Not enough to simply retire in my 30s. But it was certainly enough for this middle-class girl to feel rich, at least for a while.

It paid the bills after I left my job at the newspaper. It paid for a new green house and landscaping. It paid for trips to the Bahamas, to a luxury resort spa in Austin, Texas, and now, a trip to Hawaii, where my sister recently moved. And with not much coaxing from salesclerks, it paid for diamonds.

Who knew there was so much beautiful jewelry for sale in Hawaii?

I treated my sister to two nights at a $500-per-night resort at a dreamlike place called Kona Village Resort. She'd already spent five weeks here earlier in the year. That's how she'd used the early distribution from Dorothy's estate. She loved Hawaii so much she left her Georgia home — selling nearly everything in it — to move to the Big Island, into a condo with an expansive view of the sea.

At Kona Village, we now lounged in chairs on the black sand beach, not far from the sea turtles lazing in the sun, and talked about being heiresses.

We discussed the importance of thorough estate planning, something we each better understood after serving as executors, my sister for my parents, and me for Aunt Dorothy.

I told her I put it in my will, over the objection of my lawyer, that Henry could have control over any inheritance at age 18. My sister said she wanted her children to wait until they were 21: "I wouldn't want them to spend it frivolously."

You mean like quitting their jobs and moving to the beach?

We both burst out laughing.

And then I got silent for a moment.

I don't know... I think maybe if you have to deal with both your parents dying, you probably need to spend some of it frivolously.

She nodded. And we both stared out toward the sea turtles.

Chapter Thirty-Five

$\mathcal{L}$inda, my father's widow, was leaving me messages. I didn't return them.

For some reason, I couldn't. I wasn't sure why. Maybe it was something about her being the one who called with the worst news I'd ever received, that my dad was dying.

Linda had already called my sister who relayed the news: Linda was getting remarried. She wanted our blessing.

Oh.

It hit me like a punch in the gut.

I wasn't sure why it felt like that. Maybe it was something about the last time I saw Dad alive and well being the day he married Linda.

I loved her. She made my father happy. She deserved to be happy. She deserved my blessing.

But I avoided her calls.

I wasn't sure why. Maybe it was something about feeling like her remarriage confirmed that Dad really was no more than a memory.

How could she find another husband when I couldn't find another Dad?

I felt awful for even thinking that, but I did think it.

Finally, she caught up to me. I answered the phone and it was her. She told me the news. I acted surprised. I gave her my blessing. And then she really did surprise me.

Linda said she was getting married very soon, and could I come down to Oklahoma first. She wanted to give me her wedding ring — the one from Dad.

The ring? Oh you don't have to do that...

She insisted. And I drove down to meet her fiancé and to get the ring.

The ring was a family heirloom, a gift from my great-grandfather to my grandmother on her 18th birthday. It eventually fell into my father's possession and he gave it to Linda as an engagement ring. My great-grandfather had been a jeweler and the ring was a high-quality diamond, a full carat.

I couldn't believe I was inheriting again.

Why does this keep happening?

I hated the circumstances. I would rather my father be alive and the ring still be on Linda's finger.

She was discrete in giving it to me, sending me alone after I had met her fiancé to fetch her ring from a kitchen drawer in her house. It was there along with my father's ring, the one she had given him. I took both.

At home later, I went through my own drawers and jewelry boxes.

There was Linda's diamond ring from Dad, and Dad's white gold band from Linda.

There were two rings from Aunt Dorothy — the simple silver band she received at her wedding and a gold diamond ring she wore later.

There was my grandmother's wedding ring, the one from Dad's mother. It was another heirloom diamond.

And there was a piece I'd nearly forgotten — a star ruby ring my other grandmother received on her 50th wedding anniversary in 1969. It passed to me when she died in 1982.

Finally there was my own wedding ring, a half carat diamond I'd stopped wearing years ago.

All told, I had seven wedding rings from death and divorce. *An unmarried woman with seven wedding rings.*

I took all the rings to the bank and placed them in the safe box.

Except for one, the ring from Linda.

That one I took to the jewelry store, where I selected a new setting, a white gold band in-laid with tiny diamonds.

I should have a ring that is just mine, I reasoned.

I couldn't understand why I loved it so much. I never wanted to live rich, after all.

Maybe it had something to do with the diamond passing from father to daughter to son to wife to me.

I showed it to Henry. He shrugged and said he was sorry, he didn't find diamonds very interesting.

I told Henry where it came from. I explained the ring had been in the family for generations and would be his someday — his to give to a wife, or to a daughter.

Henry smiled.

Chapter Thirty-Six

The truck was due to arrive at the soup kitchen at 3:30 p.m. on the 2nd of October. I took Henry out of school early so he could be there to meet the truck delivering the first copies of my book from the publisher.

"Will we make it? Will we be late? I really hope we aren't late, Mommy," said Henry, as we drove from school across town to the soup kitchen.

We weren't late. The truck was.

It pulled into the soup kitchen parking lot around 4 o'clock, an hour and a half before daily dinner would be served inside. Homeless men sitting on the grass around the lot looked up to see my seven-year-old jumping up and down, screaming with delight as the back of the truck was opened.

There was my book, packed into boxes holding 70 copies each. A forklift unloaded the boxes and I immediately opened one to take a look.

Simon smiled back at me from the glossy cover, a raised paw extending out between the letters of the title, "Santa's Stray." I opened it and read the first words:

"The world is a big place.
"Millions of children live in thousands of small towns and big cities. It is hard for Santa to keep track of every boy and girl.

> *"But Santa must keep track. He wants to know not*
> *only who is naughty and nice, but who is happy*
> *and who is sad. That's where Simon comes in.*
> *"Simon is a cat. ..."*

I flipped the pages, looked over Carlene's illustrations: The one of Simon by the trash bags. The close-up of Simon's eyes. The beautiful two-page spread of Simon's neighborhood where he watches over children.

We did it, we published the book. Now we just have to sell it.

The first shipment was just part of the 10,000 we'd ordered.

Ten thousand. Henry would tell you that is 100 times 100.

I did my own mental math. Ten thousand books, three months 'til Christmas. We'd need to sell 800 a week. We'd need to sell a book to one in every 40 people in Wichita.

Could I really do that?

Angie smiled. She'd agreed to help me try.

Angie was the marketing whiz who'd gotten me on TV to promote the free Mother's Day at the botanical gardens. With her get-the-word-out skills, nearly 5,000 people showed up that day. Now she was volunteering to help sell this cat book. She believed in the cause — her husband was the architect who designed the soup kitchen — and she believed in me.

"I love this story. It's a great story!" she told me repeatedly.

Angie developed a marketing plan. She wrote press releases. She persuaded me to pose for a promotion photo, though I was camera shy and resisted until the last moment. She sent press packets to the local media. To the monthlies, the neighborhood newsletters, the radio stations, the TV stations, and my former employer, the daily newspaper. She mailed promotional materials to Oprah and Jane Pauley and Katie Couric and Regis and Kelly.

"We're going to get you on Oprah!" she insisted.

Oh jeez.

Angie set up speaking engagements, strong-armed radio talk show hosts into putting me on the air, then came along to hold my hand when I was nervous.

I told Angie she was an angel's angel.

Wendy, the soup kitchen director, handled sales. She scheduled book signings at church bazaars, an upscale gift boutique, and later, bookstores. She organized soup kitchen volunteers who delivered cases of books to their parishes. She shuttled boxes and boxes to distribution points all over town.

We collected money, $10 at a time, sometimes $20, and watched the pile of book boxes grow smaller. As word spread, we realized we were selling between 800 to 1,000 a week.

Henry came along on the book signings. He refined his sales pitch and few could resist it:

"Have you heard about The Lord's Diner?" he'd ask, stopping passersby. "It's the Wichita soup kitchen downtown that serves dinner to the hungry, 365 days a year, no questions asked."

When he had their attention, he'd point to the book on the sales table.

"This is a book my Mommy wrote to raise money for the Lord's Diner. All the money goes to the Diner. One hundred percent! This is my Mommy."

I'd smile and wave.

"It's about a cat named Simon who meets Santa on Christmas Eve and manages to grant Santa's own Christmas wish."

By now, he'd have them flipping pages, admiring the illustrations.

"And the moral of the story" — this usually got him eye contact again — "is that we all have value. Especially the least among us."

Henry proved to be an excellent salesman. Only two people who stopped to hear his full pitch ever said no to buying a book. One woman said it seemed like an excellent story and cause, but she didn't encourage her children to believe in Santa. Another woman, who stayed for a long time asking Henry lots of questions, eventually said no to him:

"Not because it's not an excellent cause. I'm just a person who really hates cats."

Chapter Thirty-Seven

*F*or days, my car had been acting up. I ignored it, thinking I was too busy with book promotions to take time out for car repairs.

A quiet day came and I finally took my car into the dealer. I described the variety of small problems, engine light sightings, etc., and sat down to wait for an estimate.

Bored, I decided to walk around. A car in the lot caught my eye.

It was a Volkswagen Beetle convertible.

I asked to see it. A salesman who said it was his first day walked me out and showed me the car.

It was loaded with features: Turbo engine, leather, heated seats, CD player, satellite radio. But the feature that interested me most was the color: The shade of blue was a dead-on match for my father's favorite car, a 1969 Ford Maverick he'd kept running through my college years.

I haggled for an hour, made a trade on my old Beetle, wrote a check for the full amount from what I like to call The Magic Checkbook and drove off in the convertible.

I picked up Henry at school, greeting him at the classroom door so I could warn him in advance. I knew he didn't like change.

Henry, I have news.

He started panicking: "ARE THE CATS DEAD?!"

No Henry, nothing like that. I bought a new car.

Henry was skeptical at first, but it was an unseasonably warm day so I took him for a ride with the top down. He put up his arms and shouted with delight: "Yesssssssss! This is like flying!"

It occurred to me, as the guilt over living rich set in again, that Mother Teresa would never buy herself a convertible. But I reasoned that if she'd ever had a chance to ride in one, she probably would have enjoyed it.

Shouldn't life be enjoyed?

It was with the belief that yes, it should be, that I took Henry out of school for a trip to Hawaii.

We went to see my sister and sea turtles and volcanoes. I taught him to snorkel. We ate pineapple. We walked through rain forests and past waterfalls. We wore flowers on our heads at a luau and turned up our noses at the octopus on the buffet. We rode a submarine 100 feet under the sea and watched tropical fish from a porthole.

Henry stood at the edge of the surf one morning. His toes dusted with black sand, he waited for the water to come wash them. The tide was gentle, and it barely lapped at his toes.

"Ah, you can do better than that!" Henry said to the sea.

His remark upset me.

Henry, never challenge the sea. You don't want to challenge the sea.

Chapter Thirty-Eight

By Thanksgiving, we'd sold more than six thousand copies of "Santa's Stray."

Nearly every media outlet Angie contacted did something on the book. But our biggest sales boost came from people who bought one book, read it, then came back for more, and sent their friends, too. Wendy predicted we'd sell 10,000 by the end of the year.

A newspaper columnist interviewed me about why I was doing this, why was I writing a children's book about strays and giving all the proceeds to charity. What was in it for me?

What's in it for me?

The columnist seemed to understand himself why a person would do this, but he wanted me to explain it for his readers. He said there were people who couldn't understand why someone would do this without some self-interest at work.

I told about wanting to be an angel, how I came from a family where if you had more than you needed, you shared. And sometimes you shared even when you didn't have enough for yourself.

My parents' families had shared during the Depression. Except for Dorothy, no one ever made much attempt to amass wealth. The measure of a person was what you gave away, not what you had.

I told the columnist I felt bad I hadn't done more; that I knew Mother Teresa wouldn't buy herself a convertible. He laughed.

What's in it for me? I'll tell you what's in for me.

My son is proud of me.

And by making him a part of this, I get to raise him in the family tradition.

As Christmas neared, Henry came home from school one day glowing. "They read "Santa's Stray" in library class today, Mommy! I think they read it to all the classes. The librarian told them my mom wrote it."

Elementary school teachers started e-mailing me, telling me they loved the book, asking me to read to their schools. One school in the poorest part of town had me come for the whole day and read to all the classes. I read the book six times that day, as sign language interpreters translated for deaf students. It was exhilarating and emotionally draining at the same time.

I decided I didn't want to do any more classes. I was worn out from the constant book promotions, the media exposure, telling my story over and over, reliving my grief. The grief, after all, wasn't all in the past. It was with me every day, as it still is.

Then a third-grade teacher sent me an email. She said she loved the book and her students had studied it in class, using it as a model for a writing assignment.

They studied it?

I told her yes, I would come. Yes, she could invite the other third-grade classes, too.

As I walked down the hall, Christmas music was playing over the intercom. It was the last day of school before winter break. The hallways were decorated with giant paper angels featuring photocopies of students' faces.

Outside the room where I was expected, Santa Claus cutouts decorated a wall. Each had a beard made of lined notebook paper, on which students had written their own Christmas stories. I stopped to read them. Many talked about strays being let in from the cold, meeting Santa and sharing secrets of loneliness.

Bits of my own soul were shining back at me in the careful pencil marks of children.

"Are you the author?"

I looked up to see the eager face of a boy, returning to his class from a trip to the restroom.

Yes, I am.

He smiled at me as I followed him in. The teacher welcomed me and summoned the two other third–grade classes. I took a seat in a director's chair and students crowded into the room, some in chairs, many on the floor.

Another eager face, right at my feet, stared up at me.

"Are you going to read us the story?"

Yes, I am.

"Oh goody, we get to hear it again! I love this story!"

It is surely impossible to feel more joy than I felt just then.

Before I read the story, I asked the students questions.

How many of you have had a stray cat?

Half the hands went up.

How many of you have had a possum get into your garage?

Laughter, and about as many hands.

How many of you have wished you had someone to play with?

Every hand up, now. Every time I ask students this question, nearly every hand always goes up — including mine. And then I tell them that I know what it's like to be lonely, how I wrote the book so more people would be understanding of people who are lonely and realize what these lonely people have to offer, if only they are given a chance.

The third–graders were good listeners as I read the story. Then they asked me questions.

"How long did it take you to write it?"

Thirty–five years of life, and one evening.

"What's the best thing about being an author?"

Reading my story to you.

"Do you still have Simon?"

Uhh... Hmm... Well...

I study their faces and make a split-second decision to tell them the truth.

Well actually, Simon died earlier this year.

They gasp.

But it was a good death. He didn't get hurt or attacked or run over.

They look relieved. (Many had already told me their strays were run over.)

And he had a great life. He gave me his story to make this book and to help feed the hungry.

I tell them the rest of the story, how Henry was crying and I said, "Who knows, maybe God will send another stray this way?" and just like that, another stray turned up and we were able to help her.

Smiles return to their faces.

"Do you still think about Simon?"

Oh yes! Every day.
Just like I think about Dad and Mom and Aunt Dorothy.
Every day.
Every single day.

Epilogue

There is no escaping the fact I am rich — in that I live in the world's richest country and I have more than I need.

In this nation, even most of our poor are rich by world standards. Rarely do our children or our elderly starve to death in the streets. Our homeless hungry are mostly men whom we expect to fend for themselves, though chronic addiction and mental illness often keep them from it.

I once wondered if my own pain and grief would keep me from fending for myself. I was afraid I would try and fail. I may still try and fail, but that won't keep me from trying.

We who are left on this earth have a responsibility to try.

In Southeast Asia, as I write this, 5 million people are trying to survive after a tsunami that washed their children into the sea, then back ashore as dead bodies littering the beaches. The death toll on this day is 120,000 and rising.

The world is trying to help. Money and food and water flowing in from an often unkind world often preoccupied with economic advantage and war. People are in shock, grieving a tragedy of this size, asking "How could God let this happen?"

I don't ask that anymore.

I understand that good people get things they don't deserve, and bad people get things they don't deserve.

I don't believe I deserved to watch my father die and then my mother and then my great aunt. Neither do I feel I deserved the money I inherited from them or the car I bought with it. But I don't look to God and say, Why did you let this happen?

And I no longer ask, Why did you leave me here in this life?

It's not God's job to answer that question. It's my job.

Circumstances are as changing as the tides: Sometimes gentle, sometimes devastating. Sometimes we may want to walk in and drown ourselves. Sometimes we may be caught off-guard and left unable to escape.

Any number of things can happen to us: We can find ourselves blessed beyond our need. We can find ourselves barely able to survive.

We should look to God, I believe, not to explain the circumstances but to help us decide how to cope with them.

As I continue to try at life, I look to the example set for me by my parents and my grandparents and my great aunt. They were loving, generous people who knew wealth wasn't to be found in money.

This is my inheritance. I am grateful.

—Polly Basore
December 31, 2004